DISAPPEARED, JAILED, AND TORTURED IN CHINA: WIVES PETITION FOR THEIR HUSBANDS' FREEDOM

HEARING

BEFORE THE

SUBCOMMITTEE ON AFRICA, GLOBAL HEALTH, GLOBAL HUMAN RIGHTS, AND INTERNATIONAL ORGANIZATIONS

OF THE

COMMITTEE ON FOREIGN AFFAIRS HOUSE OF REPRESENTATIVES

ONE HUNDRED FIFTEENTH CONGRESS

FIRST SESSION

MAY 18, 2017

Serial No. 115–31

Printed for the use of the Committee on Foreign Affairs

Available via the World Wide Web: http://www.foreignaffairs.house.gov/ or
http://www.gpo.gov/fdsys/

U.S. GOVERNMENT PUBLISHING OFFICE

25–459PDF   WASHINGTON : 2017

For sale by the Superintendent of Documents, U.S. Government Publishing Office
Internet: bookstore.gpo.gov   Phone: toll free (866) 512–1800; DC area (202) 512–1800
Fax: (202) 512–2104   Mail: Stop IDCC, Washington, DC 20402–0001

COMMITTEE ON FOREIGN AFFAIRS

EDWARD R. ROYCE, California, *Chairman*

CHRISTOPHER H. SMITH, New Jersey
ILEANA ROS-LEHTINEN, Florida
DANA ROHRABACHER, California
STEVE CHABOT, Ohio
JOE WILSON, South Carolina
MICHAEL T. McCAUL, Texas
TED POE, Texas
DARRELL E. ISSA, California
TOM MARINO, Pennsylvania
JEFF DUNCAN, South Carolina
MO BROOKS, Alabama
PAUL COOK, California
SCOTT PERRY, Pennsylvania
RON DeSANTIS, Florida
MARK MEADOWS, North Carolina
TED S. YOHO, Florida
ADAM KINZINGER, Illinois
LEE M. ZELDIN, New York
DANIEL M. DONOVAN, JR., New York
F. JAMES SENSENBRENNER, JR.,
    Wisconsin
ANN WAGNER, Missouri
BRIAN J. MAST, Florida
FRANCIS ROONEY, Florida
BRIAN K. FITZPATRICK, Pennsylvania
THOMAS A. GARRETT, JR., Virginia

ELIOT L. ENGEL, New York
BRAD SHERMAN, California
GREGORY W. MEEKS, New York
ALBIO SIRES, New Jersey
GERALD E. CONNOLLY, Virginia
THEODORE E. DEUTCH, Florida
KAREN BASS, California
WILLIAM R. KEATING, Massachusetts
DAVID N. CICILLINE, Rhode Island
AMI BERA, California
LOIS FRANKEL, Florida
TULSI GABBARD, Hawaii
JOAQUIN CASTRO, Texas
ROBIN L. KELLY, Illinois
BRENDAN F. BOYLE, Pennsylvania
DINA TITUS, Nevada
NORMA J. TORRES, California
BRADLEY SCOTT SCHNEIDER, Illinois
THOMAS R. SUOZZI, New York
ADRIANO ESPAILLAT, New York
TED LIEU, California

AMY PORTER, *Chief of Staff*   THOMAS SHEEHY, *Staff Director*
JASON STEINBAUM, *Democratic Staff Director*

———

SUBCOMMITTEE ON AFRICA, GLOBAL HEALTH, GLOBAL HUMAN RIGHTS, AND INTERNATIONAL ORGANIZATIONS

CHRISTOPHER H. SMITH, New Jersey, *Chairman*

MARK MEADOWS, North Carolina
DANIEL M. DONOVAN, JR., New York
F. JAMES SENSENBRENNER, JR.,
    Wisconsin
THOMAS A. GARRETT, JR., Virginia

KAREN BASS, California
AMI BERA, California
JOAQUIN CASTRO, Texas
THOMAS R. SUOZZI, New York

CONTENTS

DISAPPEARED, JAILED, AND TORTURED IN CHINA: WIVES PETITION FOR THEIR HUSBANDS' FREEDOM

THURSDAY, MAY 18, 2017

House of Representatives,
Subcommittee on Africa, Global Health,
Global Human Rights, and International Organizations,
Committee on Foreign Affairs,
Washington, DC.

The subcommittee met, pursuant to notice, at 2 o'clock p.m., in room 2172 Rayburn House Office Building, Hon. Christopher H. Smith (chairman of the subcommittee) presiding.

Mr. SMITH. The subcommittee will come to order, and good afternoon to everyone and welcome to our hearing this afternoon.

Lawyer Xie Yang was tortured for the better part of 2 years because he dared to represent China's poor and persecuted. The account of his detention is both harrowing and horrible.

Xie Yang was sleep deprived and kept in isolation. Squads of police punched and kicked him for hours at a time. He was forced to sit for hours on a precarious stack of plastic chairs, his feet dangling painfully off the ground. Police made threats to his wife and children and said that they would turn him into an invalid unless he confessed to political crimes.

Xie Yang and his fellow human rights lawyers wanted the best for China but what they got was the very worst. Since July 2015, almost 250 lawyers and legal assistants were detained, sending a chilling message to those fighting for legal reforms and for elemental human rights.

We are here today to shine a bright light on the brutal, illegal, and dehumanizing use of torture and forced disappearance of human rights lawyers and rights advocates in China. We shine a light on dictatorships because nothing good happens in the dark and, as we will learn today, there are some very, very dark places in China.

Chinese officials repeatedly tell us and they tell me all the time that I should focus more on the positive aspects of China and not dwell so much on the negative. That is a difficult task when you read Xie Yang's story or read Gao Zhisheng's account of his torture, and his wife and his daughter previously have testified before our subcommittee, or read the account of many other very, very brave women and men who are standing up for human rights in China.

(1)

It is a difficult task when you look at Li Chunfu and his brother, Li Heping. These are some of China's best and bravest and brightest, and now women and men with broken bodies, shattered minds, broken noses and faces, men and women who have aged 20 or more years after just 2 years or 3 of solitary confinement or torture. It is shocking, offensive, immoral, barbaric, and inhumane. It is also completely possible that Chinese officials believe the international community will not hold them to account.

While President Xi Jinping feels feted at Davos and lauded in national capitals for his public commitments to openness, his government is torturing and abusing those seeking rights guaranteed by China's own constitution and, of course, its international obligations. One Oxford University scholar said that Xi Jinping has built a "perfect dictatorship," an increasingly repressive garrison state that avoids any international censure.

Through the United Nations and the sanctions available in the Global Magnitsky Act, however, we should be seeking to hold accountable any Chinese officials complicit in torture, human rights abuses, and illegal detentions. Xie Yang identified at least 10 police officers who tortured him. We have a list of those officers who he has named. They need to be investigated by the administration and sanctions meted out individually to these individuals who have visited such horror and cruelty upon him.

We are in the process of gathering names of others as well. I, as chairman of this subcommittee, will send those names to President Trump, Secretary of State Tillerson, U.N. Ambassador Nikki Haley and the chairs and ranking members of the House Foreign Affairs and the Senate Foreign Relations Committee pursuant, again, to the Magnitsky Act protocol. We will seek U.N. investigations into the torture of China's human rights lawyers and human rights offenders. As we all know, on several occasions the Special Rapporteur for Torture has looked into the use of torture in China and has found it to be absolutely systematic.

If you are arrested and you are a religious prisoner or you are a political prisoner, a prisoner of conscience, you will be tortured and you will be tortured with depravity and with utter cruelty.

We know that this also violates China's obligations as a signatory to the U.N. Convention Against Torture. Where's the enforcement?

We will also seek investigations under the Global Magnitsky Act, as I said. I introduced the House version of that bill, which as signed into law last year. That law explicitly—and it says explicitly—that any foreign government officials who engages in or is complicit in torture can be sanctioned by denying entry visas into the United States or by imposing financial sanctions. Those who tortured Xie Yang and Li Heping should never benefit from access to the United States or to our financial system. We will hear testimony today from some of the wives who have suffered.

When a prisoner of conscience is sent off the jail and suffers it's not just that dissident who suffers. It is the wives, the families, the extended families. Very often they are rounded up as well and interrogated and beaten.

You know, we have the great Chen Guangcheng in our audience today and his wife, Beijing. When Chen suffered the barbarity of the Chinese dictatorship for speaking up on behalf of women who have been coerced into forced abortions in Linyi, he suffered in prison, then under house imprisonment. But his wife and his children also suffered and showed incredible bravery during that entire terrible ordeal. But he persevered, he persisted, and today is now free and speaks out very boldly and effectively on behalf of human rights abuses in China.

Pastor Bob Fu, who will be doing some of the translation, he too was incarcerated as a prisoner of conscience. But, again, he persisted along with his wife as well and found their way to freedom and now speaks out boldly as leader of ChinaAid.

Finally, we will hear about Mr. Li from Li Ming-Che, his wife, who will also be providing testimony to us today. After entering mainland China in March of this year for a personal trip, Mr. Li went missing for 10 days before the Chinese officials confirmed that he was being held on so-called national security grounds.

Let me just say we all know this—what a joke. People ask for human rights protections and they are accused of national security violations. It just doesn't pass the straight face test and it's about time that subterfuge and that lie, that big lie, is fully done away with and exposed.

Many fear that Mr. Li is being detained under a harsh new Chinese law to monitor and control foreign-funded NGOs enforced earlier this year as part of the crackdown on civil society.

As some of you may know, I also chair the Congressional-Executive Commission on China along with Marco Rubio, and every year we put out a very extensive account of the human rights abuses in China. One of the big changes—worsening changes—there are many—is the fact that the NGOs are now being—who had very limited freedom to begin with—have far less now just as religious organizations and denominations are also being cracked down by this cruel dictatorship.

Let me just conclude by saying that we welcome the testimony of these wives. I hope and I pray and we will monitor to ensure that because they have spoken out boldly and in a open forum like today that any further retaliation against their husbands or any members of their families will be watched closely and Xi Jinping will be noticed and I do hope the Trump administration will be bold and effective as well as Secretary Tillerson in raising individual cases, because when you raise the individual cases, obviously, it helps all the others as well.

I yield to Mr. Castro.

Mr. CASTRO. Thank you, Chairman, for your remarks and for your leadership on human rights issues worldwide.

Ranking Member Bass is unable to join us here today. I am not the superstar that she is but I am glad that she's allowed me to be the ranking member this afternoon in her absence.

Let there be no doubt that the United States will marshal its political and economic might for the cause of human rights around the world and that we will ask the same of our allies. As we move further into the digital age, information is more accessible than ever, which means that the suffering and harm to people is also more visible than ever.

The United States and nations around the world cannot turn away from what we see and we must take action. The tenure of Chinese President Xi Jinping has been accompanied by an increasingly harsh crackdown on any individuals and groups deemed to be subverting state power. The passage of the law on the management of foreign NGO activities raises serious concerns. According to the 2016 State Department report on human rights, the Chinese law describes foreign NGOs as "national security threats" and requires all NGOs to undergo a difficult registration process.

In doing so, the Chinese Government has greatly restricted the political space of its civil society. Chinese environmental activists, ethnic minorities, religious leaders, and political dissidents, among others, are routinely arrested and given years long prison sentences, often for actions as trivial as posting a comment online. And the lawyers representing these individuals often suffer equally severe treatment. Chinese human rights lawyers are routinely harassed by the Chinese security apparatus, detained for extended periods of time, tortured, charged with crimes, and sentenced to lengthy prison terms.

Last month, President Trump met with President Xi where they discussed economic and political issues. The meeting came at a time when China's crackdown on human rights reached new heights. While President Trump raised the issue of human rights with President Xi, Secretary Tillerson dismissed the idea of discussing human rights in a separate dialogue. The Secretary instead stated that U.S. core values of human rights would be part of U.S. economic or political dialogue with China.

Yet, Secretary Tillerson was the first Secretary of State who did not attend the annual release of the State Department's human rights report since the mid-1990s.

We here in Congress will pay close attention to the actions of the administration and ensure they follow through on U.S. commitments to advancing the cause of human rights in China and in nations around the world.

Today, we will hear from four brave women who continue to show their courage by testifying in front of the United States Congress. Each of their husbands has endured unjust imprisonment and inhumane treatment under dubious circumstances. They deserve our appreciation for taking great risks by providing firsthand accounts of China's increasingly restrictive political environment.

The perseverance of our witnesses and their families is a reminder that the fight for just and accountable government is a cause worth fighting for. It's also a reminder that progress toward a free and fair society is fragile and must be pursued every day.

And, of course, being a Member of Congress from Texas, I want to acknowledge that one of our witnesses has been residing there. After narrowly escaping Chinese authorities in Thailand, Ms. Chen made her way to my home state. We are happy to have you here, Ms. Chen.

Again, I want to thank each and every one of you for sharing your stories and your family stories with us today. I yield back.

Mr. SMITH. Thank you very much, Mr. Castro.

I would like to introduce our distinguished witnesses and again thank them for—thank you for your bravery and courage in coming forward.

We will begin first with Chen Guiqui, who is the wife of Christian human rights attorney, Xie Yang. Xie Yang focused his professionally life in helping those victimized by the Communist regime's forced demolitions and migrations as well as impoverished people whose rights were trampled on by the Chinese Government.

Because of his work, he was taken away on July 11th, 2015 as part of Xi Jinping's nationwide crackdown on human rights defenders. I mentioned some of the horrific ordeal that he has endured in my opening and we will hear from his wife very shortly.

We will then hear from Wang Yanfang, who is the wife of Tang Jingling, who is a human rights lawyer whose clients have included villagers fighting government corruption and victims of illegal land appropriation. In 2006, Tang's license to practice law in China was suspended, after which he became involved in a nonviolent civil disobedience movement in China.

In 2012, he was detained for 5 days following his work investigating the death of a human rights defender. In 2014, Mr. Tang was detained on suspicion of inciting subversion of state power in the weeks leading up to the 25th anniversary of the Chinese Government's violent crackdown in Tiananmen Square. He was tried in July 2015 along with two other prominent political advocates, and Ms. Wang is currently staying in the U.S. while she advocates for her husband's release.

We will then hear from Jin Bianling, wife of Jiang Tianyong. Jiang Tianyong is a veteran human rights lawyer who has worked on prominent cases including those of Chen Guangcheng and Gao Zhisheng. He has also worked on cases advocating for the rights of AIDS and hepatitis B-infected people as well as other human rights and humanitarian cases.

From 2009 to 2012, Chinese officials harassed, kidnapped and physically tortured Tang and on numerous occasions for his human rights work. In November, he traveled to Hunan to pay a visit to Chen Guiqui, the wife of the imprisoned human rights lawyer who will speak momentarily. He was kidnapped while returning to Beijing on November 21st and placed under residential surveillance for alleged subversion of state power. He is now being held.

Finally, we will hear from or we will hear from Li Ching-Yu, the wife of detained Taiwan community college worker Li Ming-Che. Ms. Li graduated from the Department of Labor Relations at the Chinese Culture University in Taiwan where she and her husband met and began to participate in social movements. Before 2014, Mr. Li began discussing Taiwan's historical experiences and issues of transitional justice with a group of Chinese friends through the instant messaging app WeChat.

In 2015, Mr. Li's WeChat account was blocked from using the group chat feature and Mr. Li began proactively seeking books as gifts to his Chinese contacts who are interested in human rights and/or modern history. Around February, 2016, he was called on friends through WeChat to raise funds for the family of a Chinese civil rights activist.

Later that year in August 2016, the books he sent to Chinese friends were confiscated. He went missing as he was entering China from the city of Macao, on March 19, 2017, so that is just a few weeks ago. Ten days later after his forced abduction, the Taiwan Affairs Office admitted he was in custody and that is why we are here today to seek his release as well.

Because we do want to hear all of you, Mr. Castro and I will take a brief respite to go vote. But we will then come back and we look forward to your testimony and I apologize for that inconvenience.

We stand in recess subject to the call of the chair.

[Recess.]

Mr. SMITH. The subcommittee will resume its sitting and I would like to yield to Randy. Randy, any comments you might have?

Mr. HULTGREN. I'll be very brief but I just wanted to say thank you for being here. Just humbled and amazed by your courage, by the stands that you are taking but also that your husbands are taking and it is so important for us to hear your stories to be able to share that with others. But also know this is, it is hard for us to still even comprehend or wrap our mind around what you are going through and what others like your families are going through.

So our hope is meetings like this, hearings like this, can encourage and push those entities that are doing these horrible atrocities to stop, to free your husbands and to make sure that this doesn't happen to anyone else's husband. So thank you for being here.

I'll look forward to hearing more of what we can do and, hopefully, seeing some positive results in very difficult circumstances.

So thank you, Chairman. I yield back.

Mr. SMITH. I thank Chairman Hultgren for coming but also for his great work that he does as chairman of the Lantos Human Rights Commission. He does wonderful work there including on human rights abuses in China. So thank you, Randy.

I would like to now ask Chen Guiqui if you could provide your testimony.

STATEMENT OF MS. CHEN GUIQIU, SPOUSE OF XIE YANG

[The following statement and answers were delivered through an interpreter.]

Ms. CHEN. Honorable Chairman Chris Smith, Honorable Subcommittee on Africa, Global Health, Global Human Rights, and International Organization Representatives, ladies and gentlemen, I am the wife of human rights lawyer Xie Yang.

I would like to thank God, the Trump administration, ChinaAid Association, and the hardworking diplomats. I also want to express my gratitude toward Representative Chairman Smith as well as other politicians and the friends who are concerned with the development of human rights and the judicial system in China.

With your help, my two daughters and I escaped from the jaws of death and arrived in the United States, the land of freedom. With your help, I am able to stand here to speak on behalf of the victims in China who do not have a voice.

I would like to give you a better idea of human rights conditions in China. And the next I will—with the help of Bob Fu to help me. So I have a request to submit the torture record of my husband

and also my husband's declaration on January 13, 2017, about his torture as part of the record.

Mr. SMITH. Without objection, all of those additions will be made a part of the record and that goes for all of our wives. Whatever it is you'd like to become a part of the record will be, without objection.

Ms. CHEN. Thank you so much. Xie Yang represented dozens of cases on behalf of the downtrodden, including poor Chinese citizens who have had their houses or land seized from them without compensation, dissidents, members of China's religious communities, and other marginalized and persecuted groups.

Due to his work defending human rights, he was jailed and brutally tortured. After Xie Yang was arrested by national security agents in Changsha and placed in secret detention for 6 months, his captors brutally tortured him attempt to make him confess and provide evidence against his colleagues.

The methods of torture included beatings delivered in rotation by a roster of guards, exhausting interrogations for over 20 hours at once, having cigarette smoke blown into his face and eyes, starvation, dehydration, and the refusal of medical treatment for his illness. To force him to surrender, his interrogators even threatened to arrange a car accident to injure his wife and children. He was beaten by a prison guard named Yuan Jin during his detention.

On November 21, 2016, his defense lawyer, Zhang Chongshi, visited Xie Yang for the first time and witnessed Yuan Jin beating him while he was waiting. Xie Yang's head swelled up and began to bleed.

Inmates who have been released from his detention center told me that he was not allowed to access money so he could not even buy toothpaste and toilet paper, not allowed to communicate with others.

He was purposely singled out. The guards specifically arranged for criminals sentenced to death to live with Xie Yang so that he would be beaten up and harassed. The publication of Xie Yang's torture account has had an immediate impact both inside China and internationally, as I just submitted today.

Xie Yang's court session was held on May 8, 2017. None of the witnesses showed up. None of the defense lawyers I hired showed up. I did not even receive a notice of the court session. Instead, Xie Yang attended the session with an official lawyer appointed by the government. The friends who planned to witness the court session were seized and arrested by the national security agents.

Xie Yang was forced to admit his guilt and deny the torture he suffered in the detention center. Regarding the fact that he was not allowed to see his lawyer for 16 months or communicate with the outside world, he was forced to acknowledge that his rights were protected. He was bailed out after the court session but still has not regained freedom. The national security agents followed him wherever he goes.

I strongly hope the Honorable President Trump and the U.S. Congress can immediately and effectively urge China's central government to investigate the actual facts behind the torture of those arrested in the 709 crackdown, simultaneously enacting legal sanctions against those who practice torture.

I request that China clearly ensures that other incarcerated prisoners of conscience do not continue to receive harm. I call on President Trump to conscientiously implement the Global Magnitsky Human Rights Accountability Act, punishing those who we have irrefutable evidence of them practicing torture and infringing on human rights.

I earnestly request that President Trump meet with the family members of the Chinese people who have suffered before he goes to China, as he's visiting with them publicly with this concern for China's worsening religious freedom, rule of law, and human rights conditions.

I also ask that he publicly give China's leaders a list of prisoners of conscience and to free the 709 case's victims.

Chen Guiqui. Thank you.

[The prepared statement of Ms. Chen follows:]

Subcommittee on Africa, Global Health, Global Human Rights, and International Organizations
U.S. House of Representatives Committee on Foreign Affairs
Disappeared, Jailed and Tortured in China: Wives Petition for Their Husbands' Freedom

Testimony of Chen Guiqiu Delivered in English by Bob Fu
Rayburn House Office Building Room 2172
Thursday, May 18, 2017

Honorable Chairman Chris Smith, honorable Subcommittee on Africa, Global Health, Global Human Rights, and International Organizations representatives, ladies and gentlemen,

I'm the wife of human rights lawyer Xie Yang.

I would like to thank God, the Trump Administration, ChinaAid Association, and the hardworking diplomats. I also want to express my gratitude toward Representative Smith and Senator Rubio, as well as other politicians and friends who are concerned with the development of human rights and the judicial system in China. With your help, my two daughters and I escaped from the jaws of death and arrived in the United States, the land of freedom. With your help, I am able to stand here and speak on behalf of the victims in China who do not have a voice. I would like to give you a better idea of the human rights conditions in China.

Xie Yang represented dozens of cases on behalf of the downtrodden, including poor Chinese citizens who have had their houses or land seized from them without compensation, dissidents, members of China's religious communities, and other marginalized and persecuted groups. Due to his work defending human rights, he was jailed and brutally tortured.

In November of 2011, Xie Yang joined many citizen activists and journalists to visit the blind lawyer Chen Guangcheng, who was under house arrest in his hometown of Linyi, Shandong. He was seized by local government-hired thugs and given a savage beating; they stole his personal belongings, ripped the clothes off his back, hooded him, then drove him to a desolate mountain roadside and dumped him in a ditch.

From 2012-2013, Xie Yang lived in the United States for one year. He gained a profound understanding of the American way of life, which made him more enthusiastic for the human rights movement in China.

After Xie Yang was arrested by national security agents in Changsha and placed in secret detention for six months, his captors brutally tortured him in an attempt to make him confess and provide evidence against his colleagues. The methods of torture included: beatings delivered in rotation by a roster of guards, exhausting interrogations for over 20 hours at once, having cigarette smoke blown into his face and eyes, starvation, dehydration, and the refusal of medical treatment for his illnesses. To force him to surrender, his interrogators even threatened to arrange a car accident to injure his wife and children.

He was beaten by a prison guard named Yuan Jin during his detention. On November 21, 2016, his defense lawyer, Zhang Chongshi visited Xie Yang for the first time and witnessed Yuan Jin beating him while he was waiting. Xie Yang's head swelled up and began to bleed.

Inmates who have been released from his detention center told me that he was not allowed to access money, so he could not even buy toothpaste and toilet paper. Not allowed to communicate with others, he was purposefully singled out. The guards specifically arranged for criminals sentenced to death to live with Xie Yang so that he would be beat up and harassed.

The publication of Xie's torture account has had an immediate impact both inside China and internationally. To name a few of the many media sources and professional organizations that covered the story or editorialized about China's lawlessness: The Washington Post, the American Bar Association, The Wall Street Journal, The New York Times, El País, Agencia EFE, The Guardian, The Irish Times, Brussels Diplomatic, and Le Monde. The European Union issued a rare statement expressing concerns over the reported torture of human rights lawyers. As a result, the Chinese national security agents in Changsha immediately summoned me, threatening and intimidating me.

Xie Yang's court session was held on May 8, 2017. None of the witnesses showed up. None of the defense lawyers I hired showed up. I did not even receive a notice of the court session. Instead, Xie Yang attended the session with an official lawyer appointed by the government. The friends who planned to witness the court session were seized and arrested by the national security agents. Xie Yang was forced to admit his guilt and deny the torture he suffered in the detention center. Regarding the fact that he was not allowed to see his lawyer for 16 months or communicate with the outside world, he was forced to acknowledge that his rights were protected. He was bailed out after the court session but still had not regained freedom. The national security agents follow him wherever he goes.

I strongly hope the honorable President Trump and the U.S. Congress can immediately and effectively urge China's central government to investigate the actual facts behind the torture of those arrested in the 709 crackdown—simultaneously enacting legal sanctions against those who practiced torture—and request that China clearly ensures that other incarcerated prisoners of conscience do not continue to receive harm. I call on President Trump to conscientiously implement the Global

Magnitsky Human Rights Accountability Act, punishing those who have irrefutable evidence of practicing torture and infringing on human rights. I earnestly request that President Trump meet with the family members of the Chinese people who have suffered before he goes to China, and, as he is visiting with them, publicly raise his concern for China's worsening religious freedom, rule of law, and human rights conditions. I also ask that he publicly give China's leaders a list of prisoners of conscience to free.

709 case victim Xie Yang's wife,

Chen Guiqiu

May 12, 2017

[*Editor's note: The following is a declaration Xie Yang wrote on Jan. 13, 2017, proclaiming his innocence*]

Xie Yang's declaration on Jan. 13, 2017

I'm Xie Yang, and I hereby declare:

Today I met with my attorney, Chen Jiangang, again. All my statements here are completely true and out of a free heart. I want to declare that I am completely innocent.

I have been suffering from all kinds of severe abuse and torture since I was arrested on July 11, 2015. Nevertheless, I have never pled guilty, because I am not guilty.

If someday I admit any guilt, whether in written form or voice recording, it would definitely not be out of my own will. It would be either caused by continued torture or to get a chance to be bailed out and reunited with my family. Both my family and I are under immense pressure now as the officials ask me to confess and stop talking about my torture.

Once again, I am innocent.

Xie Yang
Jan. 13, 2017

[*Editor's note: The following two articles were written by Chen Jiangang, Xie Yang's lawyer, and originally published and translated by China Change. The first was written shortly after a transcript describing Xie Yang's torture was published, and the second was penned when Chen began to fear that he might lose his own freedom for working on this case.*]

How Xie Yang's Transcripts of Torture Came to Light: Lawyer Chen Jiangang Rebuts China's Smear Campaign

By Chen Jiangang, March 3, 2017

1. I'm Part of the '709' Incident

I myself am an individual who's been affected by the 709 arrests and prosecutions. Sometime in late July, 2015, when I was dealing with a trial in Mengcheng, Anhui (安徽蒙城), I was taken away by state security agents on two occasions for a talking to and a warning. I was told not to do anything about the detention of lawyer Wang Yu (王宇) and others. They told me not to write articles or accept interviews. These two agents weren't malicious about it, and they even told me privately that they called me in simply to carry out the order that wherever a given lawyer happened to be, the local domestic security police would process it, and that all the information about the given lawyer was provided by Beijing. Sure enough, during the summons, I saw that the two domestic security officers had several A4 pages with my personal information on them, including that of my family.

Of course, I wasn't arrested, which was quite unexpected.

Given that I myself had been implicated in the 709 case, and because I expected that I was also going to be rounded up, I wasn't very keen on representing 709 detainees. Furthermore, I'd given up all hope in the judicial system of this tyrannical regime. The legal system in a dictatorship is simply a tool of control — it has nothing to do with justice. When the judicial system becomes a "knife handle" for the Party, human rights lawyers become helpless fish on the chopping block. As for criminal defense and its techniques, what can they be but an object of ridicule for dictators? Since my head was filled with this sort of pessimism, I didn't pay much attention to the news of Xie Yang (谢阳) being tortured. I reposted it on social media like everyone else, but avoided feeling too much pain about it, because I felt helpless. I had learned long ago that there was no evil deed, and no act too immoral, for this dictatorship. With such a sense of utter despair, I didn't even enquire about how the details of torture came out, even though later I learnt that it was Xie Yang himself who managed to get the information out of prison.

I did agree to represent lawyer Xie Yanyi (谢燕益), upon the request of his wife Yuan Shanshan (原珊珊), but he was forbidden to engage lawyers of his own choosing, and the authorities had assigned him a lawyer. I went to Tianjin twice to try to meet him, to no avail, and so I wasn't able to represent him after all.

2. About Me and Jiang Tianyong

Jiang Tianyong (江天勇) is a good friend of mine and a human rights lawyer that I have enormous respect for. He's been arrested and tortured on multiple occasions, and had eight of his ribs broken in Jiansanjiang. In Nanle county, Henan (河南南乐) in 2014, the authorities mobilized a group of village women to knock him to the ground, pelt him with rocks, bash him with a wooden stool, and rip up his clothes. And in 2011 he was slapped so savagely by state security officers that one of his eardrums was ruptured. Though we knew each other well, we didn't really stay in touch. He was always in the middle of something sensitive and hard to reach by phone. I hadn't seen him since the New Year of 2016, when we had a meal together. The last I heard from him was at some point between November 15 and 21, 2016. I published the article "Thoughts on Zhang Sizhi" (《张思之论》) on my blog on November 15. He left two comments, the first pointing out a typo and the second saying "it's an extraordinary piece." At the time I didn't know it was Jiang who'd left the message. I asked who it was, and there was no response, and by the time I found it was him, the news was out that he'd been disappeared on November 21. So it was a complete lie when Global Times claims that I was in the know when Jiang Tianyong — as the paper claims — "fabricated" Xie Yang's torture.

3. Being Hired by Xie Yang's Family

In mid-December 2016, I received a call from Xie Yang's wife. She told me that lawyer Lin Qilei (蔺其磊), one of Xie Yang's lawyers up to that point, had been forced to withdraw from the case, and that Xie hoped that I would take his case. She reminded me that I might face enormous pressure and even violent reprisal, and that I should think it over carefully. Xie Yang had been detained for 18 months and he was now personally asking me to defend him — there was no way I could I say no.

On December 19, I went to Changsha for the first time, I signed the contract with Xie Yang's wife and went to the Changsha Second Detention Center to submit the paperwork. I was working with lawyer Liu Zhengqing (刘正清); he went first to request the meeting, and I came shortly behind. I knew that there was little chance that I'd be allowed to see Xie Yang, so my job was to ensure that the paperwork was properly filed and to await their decision. If they decided that I couldn't be a defense lawyer for Xie Yang, then, just like Lin Qilei before me, there was nothing we could do but vent our frustration. The overriding role of the law in China is to be used as a tool to suppress and control the people.

The Changsha Second Detention Center rejected my documents but took down my legal license number (执业证号码) and my cell phone number. I explicitly requested that they provide an answer within 48 hours, but the officer at the reception said that he doesn't make decisions, and that the higher-ups would be handling it. I then left Changsha.

4. An Obstacle Course for a Meeting

On December 22, slightly over a month after Jiang Tianyong was taken into custody, I came to Changsha for the second time, went to the detention center, and asked to meet with my client. I first submitted the paperwork to the officer in charge of handling meetings, and he verified my legal license number and began going through the red tape. But when he saw Xie Yang's name, he said immediately: "I can't make a decision. You need to see the boss."

This officer called one of his superiors, then told me to go to the second floor to see the director. Upon seeing the director, I was told the following:

1. Meetings with clients must be conducted according to the law. They were willing to allow a meeting, but I had to obey their regulations. If any rule was violated, the meeting would be immediately terminated. He suggested that we make a gentleman's agreement, and I readily assented and assured him that I would follow the rules and that he could set his mind at ease.

2. The director suspected that on December 19 when Liu Zhengqing met with Xie Yang, I made my way to the corridor outside the meeting room without gaining the appropriate permission, and warned me that if I am to meet Xie Yang, if there is anyone in the corridor who sees or communicates with him, the meeting would be immediately terminated. I promised the director that I'd lock the door during our meetings.

For my part, I don't know what gave rise to his description of this little incident on the 19th. On that day I simply submitted the paperwork and left. I never went to the second floor where the meeting room is located, and didn't know why he thought I had. Later, I realized that the order of events was probably this: When Liu Zhengqing met with Xie Yang, they didn't close the door; one of Xie Yang's former colleagues was walking past and saw him, and then when he went back to his office he left a note about the encounter on his law firm's WeChat group, saying that he'd seen Xie Yang. Then, this was copy-pasted by another lawyer to a chat group I was in, to which I added: "I was outside at the time." Though I wasn't clear in my comment, and the "outside" I was referring to was downstairs, it was just this one little sentence that aroused the director's suspicions. And yet, how did he even know about it? In any case, this made clear to me that, as far as I'm concerned, I have no such thing as privacy. This incident was proof of it.

3. After meeting with the director, I thought Xie Yang and I would be able to meet. But no. The officer at the reception told me that I had to speak with the deputy director of the detention center. I then went back to the second floor and received another round of warnings from the deputy director, who rattled off a bunch of policies and how they were all for the good of Xie Yang and so on.

After these three obstacles, I was finally able to meet Xie Yang.

5. The First Meeting With Xie Yang

Xie Yang and I met at about 10:30 a.m. on December 22, 18 months after he was detained. His hair was getting long and he had grown a beard. He was clearly dispirited. He was escorted in wearing the blue prison uniform, carrying his case files, with a guard on either side. When he saw me his face lit up: "Jiangang, you came!" He was seated, his handcuffs taken off and placed on a stool, and as the two officers left I asked them to close the door because the room was freezing.

When the police left, I cupped my hand with a fist and said to Xie Yang: "Brother, you've suffered!" He asked how I came; I explained that I'd just been in Jinan sitting in a hearing about the suspension of Li Jinxing's (李金星) law license, and that Wen Donghai (文东海) bought me a train ticket to come here, and that I came with Old Sui (隋牧青), who's waiting outside. When I got this far, Xie Yang broke into tears. The fact that so many people outside were thinking of him and worrying about him moved him deeply.

We exchanged thoughts about the 709 affair. He said he'd seen the forced confession of Zhou Shifeng (周世锋), and roughly knew the circumstances of Wang Yu and others. I said that "of all the lawyers arrested in the 709 crackdown, you're the only one to be represented by his own attorney." He replied: "Then I need to save a final bit of dignity for lawyers in China!" These words he spoke through tears, and we grasped one another's hands through the iron grating, both of us now crying. The time passed quickly and it was soon noon. We agreed to continue that afternoon.

In the afternoon I went to the court with Xie Yang's wife to submit the paperwork for me to be registered as the lawyer of record, then hurried to the detention center to meet again. Xie Yang and I discussed case defense strategies and ideas. He was very self-confident, and wanted to explain the truth of everything in court, to set the whole case out for all to see. But I was full of sorrow. Can we actually do that? Can we, brother?

Let me pause and explain the layout of the meeting room.

The room we met in was called the "No. 2 West Meeting Room," and it was given over for Xie Yang's exclusive use. The police in charge of the administrative procedures for meetings had come and stuck up a sign saying "Reserved for Xie Yang Case." To the right and left behind where I was seated there were cameras, and then there was another, above left, facing me — those were the three cameras that I could see. Because of the director's warning, as soon as I entered the meeting room, I locked the door. When another lawyer, having left an electronic swipe card in the room, came back to retrieve it, I handed it to him through the window rather than open the door and break the gentleman's agreement between myself and the director. Before I entered the room, I placed my cell phone and briefcase in the storage cabinet as required. However, I found that not every lawyer was held to this requirement. Many others brought their briefcases in, or would speak on their phone as they mounted the stairs. But I didn't dare.

The surveillance of our meetings was extremely strict. On one occasion the door on Xie Yang's side suddenly opened and a police officer came in, saying that on the monitor Xie Yang's mood didn't seem right, and "has he been crying?" Another time,

Xie Yang wrote down the phone number of his former legal assistant, asking me to pay back, as soon as possible, a few thousand yuan that he had borrowed before he was arrested. I looked at the number, then thought that I could get it later another way, so I gave the slip of paper back to him. But this exchange was caught by the cameras, and two police came in and demanded the paper that Xie Yang had shown me. They grabbed all the case files on both sides of the grating, dumped them on tables, and began searching through them. When I was leaving that day the deputy director of the facility asked me specifically about this incident, and I told him the truth: Chinese New Year was nearly upon us, Xie Yang owed this person money, if he didn't pay it back it would bother him to no end, so he asked me to pay them back.

After this incident, whenever Xie Yang or I made to look at materials or case files, I would hold the paper up above my head to ensure that the cameras got a clear view. If the police monitoring the conversation still objected they could come in anytime and see for themselves.

One time, one of the police at the reception, after seeing me coming to visit every morning and afternoon, remarked "It doesn't look to me like you're up to anything — you're just chatting!" Right — just chatting. If we didn't just chat, how would I have been able to find out all that happened over the last 18 months?

6. A Rough Transcript of the Interview on December 23, 2016

We continued our meetings on December 23. Having just looked up the notes I made after that meeting, I append them below largely unaltered. Xie Yang said to me: "Jiangang, let me tell you roughly what happened after I was detained. Don't make notes. Just listen so you'll know the outline, and then we'll go over it in detail." I made notes, stopping now and then and asking him for clarification. He'd always say, "Let me talk first, then we we will go into details." I did make some initial notes as he spoke, which would serve as the basis for my interview with Xie Yang on January 4-6, 2017. They are as follows:

> On July 11, 2015, I was staying at a hotel while traveling for a case. In the early morning hours, there was a knock at the door. A voice said that it was public security police. I opened the door, and they presented me with a summons for "gathering a crowd to disturb order in the workplace" (聚众扰乱单位秩序). The agency that issued the summons was the Hongjiang Municipal Public Security Bureau.
>
> They brought me to their station, whereupon agents from public security in Changsha carried out the interrogation. They asked what my views were on Wang Yu's case, whether I'd accepted interviews with foreign media, and so on. At this point I objected. They kept me locked up and, later, they came to coax me, and I signed a transcript of the session.
>
> In the afternoon, a superior named Li Kewei (李克伟) came and said that my answers were superficial and that I had to redo it. I refused.

They kept me there, and in the evening took me to the Changsha Public Security Bureau.

Li Kewei demanded my cell phone password. He'd been threatening me constantly, from when we got on the road from Hongjiang to Changsha, saying that my case is a big one, that they're representing Party Central in handling it, and if I don't cooperate then my wife, my parents and siblings, friends, and everyone around me will all be implicated. I said that you can investigate me or anyone you want.

As soon as we got out of the car in Changsha two police came along, one named Zhou Liang (周浪), the other Yin Zhuo (尹卓). They took me to room 207 of the National University of Defense Technology's (国防科技大学) guesthouse for retired cadres. By then it was the afternoon of July 12. Wang Tieta (王铁铊), the head of the Sixth Squadron at the Changsha Domestic Security Bureau, came to speak with me. He began by making threats. He said that he could guarantee that I would get "reasonable" rest, but that unfortunately there was no legal definition for what counted as "reasonable." So, in his words, "If we think that two hours sleep a night is reasonable, then it's two hours sleep. If we think that one hour is enough, then it'll be one hour. If we think that 20 minutes suits you, then it'll be 20 minutes." I got to sleep at about midnight that night.

I was rousted out of bed at 6:30 a.m. to be handed off to the first of five interrogation shifts they had set up. The first shift had me from 8:00 a.m. to 1:00 p.m.; the second from 1:00 p.m. to 6:00 p.m.; the third from 6:00 p.m. to 11:00 p.m.; the fourth from 11:00 p.m. until 3:00 a.m. These were the first four teams. The fifth was from 3:00 a.m. to 8:00 a.m., but they didn't interrogate. Along with these main shifts of interrogation there were three shifts of chaperons, two people each shift, working on eight hour rotations.

The number of police in each shift wasn't fixed. Sometimes it was two, sometimes three, sometimes five. But only two people signed off on anything. They would ask me about what I'd written. I said that anything I've got to say is posted online, and they can look it up for themselves — it's all public. They took turns interrogating me.

The fourth shift was supposed to go from 11:00 p.m. until 3:00 a.m., but Yin Zhuo liked to question me until 4:00 or 5:00 a.m. I was woken up every day at 6:00 a.m., so I got about over an hour of sleep a night.

Yin Zhuo said to me in front of the others: "I've come especially to make your life hell. I sleep very well during the daytime, and when night comes I'm going to torture and torment you until you lose your mind." At that moment, a sense of dread seized my heart. I had no idea what would happen. This sleep deprivation lasted three days, and by then I was about to fall apart. When they asked about my friends, I was so exhausted that I simply cried.

Yin Zhuo said that lawyer Zhang Lei (张磊) had been arrested right after his wife had a baby. They also threatened my own family. I just lost it and cried and cried.

Until about July 15 or 16, they forced me to make a list of every person I had contact with from the 2012 to 2015, and which cases I was involved in. I had to put it all down in detail. I was so exhausted that I said I simply couldn't do it.

Three or four of them, including Yin Zhuo, Zhou Liang, and Zhuang Xiaoliang (庄晓亮), came in, pinned me to the table, twisted my hands behind my back and cuffed them, then began pounding me. The door and windows of the room I was being kept in were shut tight. They said that I could yell all I wanted. There was no one around, and no one would hear me scream.

When Yin Zhuo and Zhou Liang were interrogating and torturing me, the officers in the chaperon shift would leave. When they were done, Yin Zhuo would tell them to come back and make sure I didn't fall asleep. They sat and stared at my eyes, and if I shut them they'd come and shake my chair. I couldn't get any rest all night, and a whole day would pass in this manner.

I said: "If you keep this up, you're going to kill me. The case against me is just a case — you should at least have some humanity." On July 16 they let me sleep for an hour or two, just so I'd be able to write for them when I woke up. I told them that I'd written everything I could, and that I don't remember everything over the past two years, and that I'd rather die.

They took out my phone and computer and started looking through the messages I'd posted to chat groups and friend circles, because I have a habit of sending out updates of what I'm doing and which cases I'm handling. They told me to write all that down. When I was done, they said it was not good enough. So they kept torturing me.

Zhuang Xiaoliang said: "It's mainly up to your attitude. Your case is big — the No. 1 case. Do you think this is a mistake and that you can go to Beijing and lodge a complaint against us? Do you think Beijing doesn't know what we're doing to you? If we want to hurt you, we can do what we like." Both Yin Zhuo and Zhuang Xiaoliang said this sort of thing.

I was facing the threat of death. When they beat me, they would drag me away to a blind spot for the cameras and slug me hard. Sometimes they beat me in front of the cameras. I wondered if they were going to beat me to death, then fake a scene so it looked like I'd killed myself.

After five or six days of this I was basically paralyzed. I couldn't open my eyes, and my entire body throbbed in pain. I told them that I would write whatever they wanted, and I'll sign whatever they wanted me to.

They looked up some of the case information related to Zhou Shifeng and Zhai Yanmin (翟岩民) and forced me to write that out. I wrote whatever they said. That's how those interrogation transcripts came about.

During the six months I was locked in that guesthouse, they beat me like that on about five or six occasions. They also used other torture, such as the "dangling chair" (吊吊椅). That's where they would stack up plastic stools and make me sit on top so that my feet would hang there. They made me sit like that every day for over a month during the interrogations. My legs eventually swelled up, starting at the calves and going up to the thighs. I couldn't even walk at the time. They basically turned me into a cripple.

I asked that they take me to the Liuyang Orthopedic Hospital (浏阳骨 科医院), because I was worried that this abuse would leave me with a permanent injury. They refused. Instead they gave me a little spray canister of Yunnan Baiyao [a traditional Chinese medicine], and after about a month the swelling went away.

There was another torture, using smoke. They would sit people behind, in front, and to the left and right of me, and each of them would have four or five lit cigarettes in the hand, burning away. Then they would blow the second-hand smoke into my face, making me weep, gag, and suffocate. They would do this to me at 3:00 or 4:00 a.m. each day, torturing me. I screamed out to Heaven and Earth for help, to no avail.

They also refused to give me water. They said: "We'll give you water whenever we feel like it." They would often not give me water for over 10 hours at a stretch.

They did a number of things to deliberately torment me. They'd leave hot food to go cold before letting me eat. For example, they would leave lunch on the floor until 2:00 or 3:00 p.m., then serve it to me cold.

They used all of these methods for the first week or so, and after that, having found it quite effective, they canceled the later two shifts.

During the later interrogations, if they didn't like my attitude they'd threaten me: "Xie Yang, do we need us to put you back in the oven?" Or they would say: "Xie Yang, if we want to kill you, it would be very simple. Killing you is the same as killing an ant!"

I had terrible constipation, and needed fruit to relieve it. They used this to blackmail me. They would make me write things, and only if they were happy would they give me fruit. When I couldn't write, they would type it up on a computer, print it out, and make me sign it.

On October 24 my whole body shook. I don't know why. I had a cold sweat, and started to get extremely scared about my condition. I told them that I needed to go to hospital. They reported to Ye Yun (叶云, political commissar of the Changsha Domestic Security Bureau's Sixth Squadron), who came and said that he couldn't allow that, but could arrange for medics to come examine me. I didn't trust their doctors, so I ran to the window and screamed out: "I'm Xie Yang, a lawyer, I've been locked up here by the Changsha domestic security police! They haven't told my family! Please tell my wife that I'm sick and need medical treatment!" There were people walking past, and I yelled out my wife's name, work unit, and phone number, and told the pedestrians to call her.

That night at 9:46 p.m. Ye Yun used his cell phone to call 120. [China's emergency service]

While waiting for first aid to arrive, a large, physically powerful man turned up. He was not wearing a uniform. He used one hand to pin me to the wall, and the other to slap me hard across the face, forehand and backhand, again, and again, and again. The pressure on my chest alone was unbearable. I couldn't speak and could hardly breathe, and on top of that I was being pounded in the head. He knocked me half unconscious.

About 20 minutes later the ambulance came. First, domestic security wouldn't let them examine me, and called them outside for a word. Later, a young medic surnamed Wang came in and inspected me — a very cursory examination. There was no treatment, no medication. He just said "the case requires further observation" and left.

Yin Zhuo brought me to a place in the apartment outside the view of the camera and said: "Xie Yang, you've been a lawyer for only three years. You couldn't have done too many wicked things even if you did it every day, so all you have to do now is implicate Yang Jinzhu (杨金柱) and Cai Ying (蔡瑛), and we'll release you on bail. This is what the boss says." He went on and on trying to talk me into it.

I said that I had little contact with Yang Jinzhu, I'd only eaten a meal and had a drink with Cai Ying, and that I had no idea what they'd done.

They also wanted me to implicate more lawyers involved in the Jiansanjiang incident. They promised me that if I implicated others, I would be released on bail, and that reporting malefactors is recognized by law as "merit," and so on.

No matter how much they wanted me to write this, I wouldn't write it. I cannot harm other people. They said that they can just write it themselves and have me sign it. I told them not to do that, and that I haven't even had much contact with those people. They showed me a letter that Liu Jinbin (刘金滨) had written to me.

The above are the notes I made while listening to Xie Yang on December 23. I left Changsha that night.

7. Making the First Transcript of Interviews

I made the first transcript of the interviews from January 4-6, 2017.

Let me first discuss the connection between myself and Liu Zhengqing. Old Liu and I have known each other for years, but this was the first time we worked together on a case, and Xie Yang is a mutual friend and colleague. Xie Yang thought highly of my writing skills and urged me to be the first defense counsel, and to work together with Old Liu. Old Liu is half bald, and the hair that's left is grey. His face looks like it's seen an age, like he's over 70. All this imperceptibly adds to his prestige and the power of his speech. Actually, he's the same age as lawyer Zhao Yonglin (赵永林) — they were both born in 1964.

We agreed that Old Liu would take care of filing complaints, while I'd be the one to write them up. Xie Yang is a stubborn fellow — if he wants to do something, I can't talk him out of it. I'm the younger one in the relationship, and will oblige the older one — not the other way around. This is where Old Liu came in handy.

Xie Yang's wife knows his character very well, and she knows that Old Liu is able to overpower Xie Yang. On the afternoon of January 4, I went in first to see Xie Yang while Old Liu went to the court to hand over the paperwork. After that he came to join me in the No. 2 West Meeting Room at the detention center. Xie Yang was in a rage at the police falsifying evidence and lying, and he was about to blow up. At the meeting room, Xie Yang and I were talking, Old Liu said to Xie Yang: "Listen to me, Xie Yang. You've got to listen to our advice. Don't act rashly. You've been locked up for a year and a half, and you don't know what's going on on the outside. Don't think that you're so great. Right now your wife has left a far better impression on the world than you. Your wife said that if you didn't listen to us, she'd dismiss Jiangang and not let him come anymore...." Xie Yang fell silent for a good while. In the end, he mumbled reluctantly: "I authorized my wife to engage or fire lawyers, as a way of resisting government designating lawyers for me, not as a way to contain me...." But in the end Xie Yang accepted our ideas.

We then started working on the transcript. Old Liu sat by, I asked questions, and Xie Yang answered, one after another. The surveillance cameras should have caught the entire process very clearly.

From the afternoon of the January 4th (Wednesday) until Saturday afternoon, we made the transcript. Because of the character input method I was using, it was easy to input time — I hit 's' and 'j' and it would give a timestamp, so I'd output the time at the beginning and end of the sessions.

Men don't cry easy. But over those three days, Xie Yang and I both shed tears regularly, again showing the effect of an evil system in destroying human nature, as well as the sins and tragic brutality that come along with government power that acts with impunity. During the sleepless nights that followed I would recall scenes from our conversation. Xie Yang, in his prison garb, mussed hair, scraggly beard, exhausted with no lustre in his eyes, described how he worried that he'd be beaten to death and that his family wouldn't know where he died. As he wept, I reached out to him and began weeping too. When describing how the security agent Yin Zhuo and others threatened the lives of his wife and daughter, saying they were going to stage a car accident to kill them, Xie Yang cried again. I stopped typing and thumped the table hard and repeatedly with a closed fist.

By Friday morning the transcript of the first interview was finished, and Xie Yang I went over it. After lunch I made a copy at a copyshop outside the detention center and asked Xie Yang to sign it when I saw him in the afternoon.

This was how the first transcript came about.

8. Making the Second Transcript of Interviews

On January 12 to 13, 2017, Xie Yang and I met again, and again transcribed the interviews. The Q and A process was again all carefully captured by the surveillance cameras in the room. On the afternoon of January 13, Xie Yang verified the transcript with a signature.

It's worth noting that when I arrived for our January 13 meeting, I carried 5-8 visitation permit letters in a folder as I always did. I left the folder in the storage cabinet, but when I came back in the afternoon, they had all vanished. I broke out into a cold sweat — without these letters, I couldn't visit Xie Yang, and every visitation usually requires several letters. Every time I left for a meeting, I would check twice to make sure. Where were they? I checked to see if there were any surveillance cameras with a view of the storage cabinet, and it seemed there were none. I asked one of the police officers whether there was a camera with a view of the cabinet, and he rebuffed me with: "If you've got a problem go ask the boss. I don't know anything."

I was just so fortunate, however, to have one last letter, left over from a visit in the Weihai detention center in Shandong. I found it in a courier envelope. This letter saved me. Xie Yang and I successfully met on the afternoon of the 13th, and he signed off on the transcript.

Later, I was mulling it over: is it me who forgot where I put the visitation letters? Or was it something else? On February 28, when Liu Zhengqing came to Changsha and requested a meeting, he was rejected. The reason was explicit: you're not allowed to meet because the special investigation team has taken Xie Yang away for interrogation. Interrogation has no time limit, and there's no time allocated for a meeting with lawyers. During all this back and forth, a black satchel of Liu's also mysteriously went missing. Once I heard this, I no longer wondered about the reasons for the disappearance of those visitation letters of mine.

9. The Lies of the *Global Times*

Global Times has no shame. Its article "Exposing the truth behind the 'torture of Xie Yang': Making up lies to pander to the West" (《揭秘"谢阳遭酷刑"真相：为迎合西方凭空捏造》) didn't even have a byline. If there's no byline, how can anyone be held accountable? Who takes responsibility for the truth and accuracy of the reporting? Only garbage media without any sense of shame behave in this manner.

I am an independent lawyer. I work and operate freely and independently. I am not subject to the manipulation or constraints of anyone, and I take full responsibility for the accuracy of every character of the transcripts that I have made and published. *Global Times* has concocted far too many fake stories, so it thinks that other people do the same. It doesn't seem to know that truth does exist.

Though Jiang Tianyong and I are good friends, he wouldn't make up rumors and have me repeat them. Nor would I ever do that. Just because *Global Times* "reports" by following political directives doesn't mean everyone else is doing the same.

The last time I saw Jiang Tianyong it was two or three days after New Year's day in 2016, when he, Li Jinxing (李金星) and a few others went out to eat. I hadn't seen him since then. Our communication, whether via phone or email, had been even sparser. He hardly ever answered the phone, didn't use WeChat, and was hard to get ahold of in person. I'm also not used to getting around the internet firewall on my smartphone, so there are almost no communication records between us. It was only after he was apprehended that I found the two messages he'd left for me. The date was between November 15 and November 21. *Global Times* has no shame when it claims that Xie Yang's defense lawyer [me] and Jiang Tianyong fabricated claims of torture.

Global Times is a Party mouthpiece. It has nothing to do with truth and everything to do with propaganda.

10. The Phoenix Television Interview of Jiang Tianyong and Xie Yang

I have the greatest sympathy for the plight and vulnerability of Jiang Tianyong who, in the hands of those scum, can't control his own fate. Jiang Tianyong was tortured on numerous occasions, and he made multiple statements denigrating himself. Having experienced the barbaric torture first hand, he told friends that, if he's tortured, he may very well submit to their demands, because the methods they use are beyond what any human can withstand. An examination of Xie Yang's testimony makes this clear. Thus, I feel for Jiang Tianyong in the same manner that I feel for Wang Yu and others. They are brave warriors, they are victims of a tyranny, and they are the light of dawn at the end of the night.

In all of the interviews Xie Yang gave, he never denied the torture he experienced. Xie Yang said that when he demanded someone call 120 for a doctor, it was due to his own illness, not because he'd been beaten. That's what he said in the interview, and it does not negate the fact that he was tortured.

He said on camera that he now gets about nine hours sleep a night, and this seems to be the situation currently — but it does not negate the torture he suffered during the six months of "residential surveillance at a designated location" a year ago. Also, he repeatedly said that the improvement in his conditions of detention was because his lawyers lodged a complaint against abuse, not because the detention center has always been so generous.

It's similar to when researchers say that during the great famine of 1958, millions died, and then the fifty-cent commentators say that in the year 2000 everyone can afford to eat their fill. Are these two things related? Does one negate the other?

Xie Yang is now healthy and can walk and climb stairs normally — but do these facts have any logical relation to the six months of torture he experienced after July 11, 2015? Does the fact that he can climb stairs now negate the fact that he was subjected to severe sleep deprivation?

Xie Yang seems talkative in the *Global Times* interview. He might have spoken about the torture and then the improvement, except that he was not informed of the cynical use of the interview. I'd be surprised if *Global Times* has any credibility anywhere in the world.

11. The Hunan Procuratorate's 'Investigation'

The so-called investigation by the Hunan Procuratorate was neither fair nor just. In totalitarian China, all of the powers of the judicial, procuratorial, police, and public security organs are one, and those in power can do whatever they want. In Xie Yang's case, he was accused of the crime of opposing the Party and opposing socialism. The investigation was conducted by the Party, the review was carried out by the Party, the trial will also be presided over by the Party. Now that Xie Yang's torture has become an international scandal, the investigation was again done under the leadership of the Party. Everything is handled by the Party — in other words the Party is the player and the referee at the same time. This scandalous power structure is sacred in China and must be preserved and praised. It's always for repression, never for truth, fairness, or justice. The "investigation" then is a coverup, and another attack on Xie Yang and his defense counsel.

Let's examine their facile logic. One of the prosecutors said they did an experiment: they found someone who was slightly shorter than Xie Yang, sat him on a stack of five plastic stools, and found that his feet could still reach the ground, supposedly thus proving that Xie Yang was lying.

In Xie Yang's transcript, he said they used "a number of plastic stools stacked atop one another," and that he was forced to sit on top, "leaving my legs to dangle." Did he specify how many stools were used and the size of the stools? If 5 stools were too short for feet to dangle from, would 10, or 20 be high enough?

12. The Surveillance Camera

The evidence with the most probative value, of course, is that which is recorded by video camera. According to a long-standing law, individuals charged with political crimes must have their interrogations recorded. But in Xie Yang's case files, there is no surveillance recording, and in its place is a note by the investigators: "Due to the decrepitude of the equipment, there was no recording of the interrogation." If the equipment was not functional, then you shouldn't have conducted the interrogation. Has anyone been sold on these shameless lies?

13. Gratitude to Lawyer Zhang Zhongshi

One individual I have come to respect deeply when dealing with 709 cases is lawyer Zhang Zhongshi (张重实). I can't match his exertions, and I couldn't bear what he regularly withstands. Zhang Zhongshi was the first defense attorney that Xie Yang's wife hired. His law firm and family are in Xiangtan (湘潭), Hunan. He's traveled from Xiangtan to Changsha over 100 times to take care of Xie Yang's case. He visited every single related government office, and on each occasion affected a respectful, solicitous demeanour, quietly putting up with their insults and bullying, all for the purpose of just being able to meet his client, Xie Yang. So-called "residential surveillance at a designated location" should not be a black jail; the detainee should be able to freely meet their own attorneys and family members — but the lawyers have been stripped of all these rights. After six months in a black jail, Xie Yang was formally arrested, but still the authorities prevented his meeting with lawyers in the name of "endangering state security," and "interrogation by prosecutors."

Xie Yang's wife told me that on one occasion, a junior police officer clad in a black uniform looked at Zhang Zhongshi and rebuked him: "You're a lawyer but you don't know the law?" But Zhang didn't return fire on this upstart, who was young enough to be his son or daughter. He simply kept the smile on his face and patiently explained what the law actually stipulates. I couldn't have done this. Xie Yang couldn't have done it. Many of us couldn't have done it.

Zhang Zhongshi was not alone. Lawyer Cheng Hai (程海) in Beijing, lawyer Lin Qilei, lawyer Yu Wensheng (余文生), and lawyer Ma Lianshun (马连顺) in Henan, as well as others, have all persevered and persisted. I have to acknowledge that I couldn't have done what they have done.

To lawyer Zhang, I give my gratitude — and so does Xie Yang.

Chen Jiangang

March 2, 2017

'In the Event That I Lose My Freedom': A Statement by Lawyer Chen Jiangang

By Chen Jiangang, March 4, 2017

1.   I cherish life. I want to live to see the universal values of democracy, liberty, rule of law, and human rights realized in China. I want to see a constitutional system of government established in China. If these things don't happen I'll die without peace. I cherish my family. I want to see my children grow and live in freedom and health. For all these reasons, I will not kill myself. If something unexpected happens to me, please know that it will absolutely not be because I committed suicide.

2.   I have committed no crime. I will never, of my own volition, assent to any illegal interrogation, and nor will I level false charges against or attempt to frame anyone. Any written, oral, or video confession, self-degradation, or accusation against other people will only have been made under the circumstances that I have been deprived of liberty, am under duress, or am being tortured and threatened. Those are the only circumstances under which I could be forced to say such things, and none of them will be true.

3.   I'm simply a man of flesh and blood. If I'm put to the agonies of torture, I cannot guarantee that I will not submit. Through my years of work as a defense lawyer, I have learned of many cases of torture in China and the unspeakable cruelty involved. If I am tortured and made to submit, everything I say will be made up. None of it can be taken as evidence toward the accusation, conviction, or defamation of any person.

4.   If I lose my freedom and end up on television revealing the name of any of my friends, please forgive me. Those won't be my own words or my will. By that stage I will have been turned into nothing but a prop. Please forgive me.

5.   I take complete responsibility for every character in the two transcripts I made of the meetings with Xie Yang (谢阳), as well as for any other transcripts that have not yet been made public. As for the groundless lies made by the shameless state media that the transcripts describing torture were fabricated, I have already thoroughly rebutted them in my essay "How Xie Yang's Transcripts of Torture Came to Light."

6.   My children, your father loves you.*

Chen Jiangang (陈建刚)

2017-03-03

*Chen Jiangang has two children, six and two years old.   – Translator's note

———————

Mr. SMITH. Ms. Chen, thank you so very much for your testimony and, again, for you and all of the wives for your bravery.

We'd like to now ask Wang Yanfang. So Ms. Wang.

STATEMENT OF MS. WANG YANFANG, SPOUSE OF TANG JINGLING

[The following statement and answers were delivered through an interpreter.]

Ms. WANG. Honorable Chairman Smith, Honorable Subcommittee on Africa, Global Health, Global Human Rights, and International Organizations representatives, ladies and gentlemen, my name is Wang Yanfang, wife of human rights lawyer, Tang Jingling.

I would like to express my gratitude to Representative Chris Smith, Senator Marco Rubio, Representative Nancy Pelosi, Representative Hultgren, and many other Representatives, as well as Bob Fu, president of ChinaAid Association, for your attention to and support of my husband and many other victims of human rights abuse in China. I would like to request the committee to archive my husband's report on the violation of human rights in Chinese prisons. The rest of my testimony will be read by Jasmine Chia Shih.

As the institution of religious freedom, rule of law, and human rights continues to deteriorate in China, support for the victims of the international community is very valuable and precious.

This is also an important milestone in joint endeavors to maintain universal values all over the world. In the past few decades, people of many countries terminated their seemingly powerful and long-lasting autocratic regimes through nonviolent resistance and fulfilled the transition from autocracy to democracy.

My husband is a well-known human rights lawyer. He is also the initiator and a keen advocate of the civil disobedience movement. He is dedicated to promoting the civil disobedience movement, hoping to bring forth a democratic and free China. In 1995, the national security police began to monitor Tang Jingling after he expressed his lifelong mission to promote democracy in China. In 1999, he published an article on China's democratization in Guangzhou. Then, he was forced to leave the big law firm he was working for.

As a human rights lawyer, he's been involved in many major cases of human rights abuse, political rights abuse, and workers' rights abuse. For example, in 2003, a petition was initiated to abolish the internment and repatriation regulations and cancel the temporary residence permits policy after college student Sun Zhigang's death. Tang Jingling served as the legal counsel. In 2004, he was the defense lawyer for the two people charged in the Xingang labor unrest case in Dongguan.

In January 2005, he defended the newly elected village head in the Shibi Third Villagers' campaign to remove old village officials. In August 2005, he was one of the key lawyers in the case of the Taishi villagers' campaign to remove village officials. Due to his involvement in human rights cases, the authorities forced his law firm to terminate his employment and suspended his lawyer's license.

In 2006, he planned to attend an event in the U.S., but he was stopped at customs and his passport was confiscated by the police. He's still not allowed to leave the country to this day. After losing his lawyer license, he participated in many human rights cases as a citizen, including the poisonous vaccine lawsuit, the investigation of Li Wangyang's death, and many other cases involving land property, forced demolition, and so on.

My husband graduated from Shanghai Jiaotong University in 1993. He began to participate in law in 1998. He lost his lawyer license in 2005. Due to his work in human rights protection during the Jasmine Movement in February 2011, he was charged with inciting subversion of state power and was detained in a black jail where he was threatened and tortured, including extensive sleep deprivation for 10 days in a row. He was allowed to sleep for 1 to 2 hours a day after he began to have some dangerous symptoms like trembling all over, numbness in both hands, and heart discomfort until he was released on August 2, 2011.

He initiated and promoted the civil disobedience movement to seek justice for people at the bottom of the society. But his wife was forced to lose her job in May 2008.

During his detention in February 2011, I was forcibly brought to Conghua and detained. They took my phone, bruised my arms, and didn't allow me to notify my family and lawyer, which caused my severe depression and poor health. Then the police tricked my mother to go to Guangdong to take care of me, and I was put under house surveillance for a long time. I was not allowed to meet with any family and friends. I was not even allowed to leave my home. More than 20 people took turns watching me. I was completely isolated from the outside world for almost 5 months. When my husband was released, my physical and mental health had been severely damaged.

On May 16, 2014, Tang Jingling was criminally detained on the charge of "picking quarrels and provoking troubles" and was arrested on June 20 with the charge of "inciting subversion of state power."

On September 23, his mother passed away on hearing of his arrest. His lawyer and I applied to bail him out to attend his mother's funeral. But the authorities ignored everything on legal, moral, and humanitarian levels and rejected our request. They didn't notify him of her death until October and caused deep sorrow. The authorities forbade his lawyer to meet with him for 6 months while his case was being transferred to the procuratorate.

During the 2 years in the detention center all communication was banned. There was no way to guarantee his rights.

On January 29, 2016, he was sentenced to 5 years imprisonment with the charge of inciting subversion of state power. He's serving the sentence in Huaiji Prison, Guangdong Province.

Since he was arrested in August 2013, I was put under 24-hour surveillance, which brought huge emotional pressure and fear to me. However, I've been appealing for my husband. I request the release of him.

On July 1, 2014, I went to Hong Kong to attend a demonstration and appealed in the media to urge people to pay attention to Tang Jingling and other prisoners of conscience like Yuan Chaoyang and

Wang Qinqying. I was threatened by the police after returning to Guangdong and my freedom was restricted during the so-called "sensitive" period. After the massive arrest of human rights lawyers on July 9, 2015, I got in touch with families of arrested human rights lawyers and went to the Supreme People's Procuratorate with them.

In August, I was not allowed to leave home. Since Tang Jingling worked as a lawyer more than a decade ago, he participated in many human rights cases and promoted civil disobedience movement. Consequently, he lost his lawyer license. He was detained, monitored, arrested, tortured and sentenced, and I lost my job, was harassed, summoned, monitored, and detained.

Today, other 709 case lawyers are still suffering from such torture. Many prisoners of conscience are still unable to meet with their lawyers and families. Christian churches are still being shut down. Christians are still being detained and sentenced.

Thus, I sincerely plead with President Trump and the U.S. Congress to urge the Chinese Government guarantee Tang Jingling's right to meet with his lawyer and his right to reading, communication, medical treatment, and food with enough nutrition as well as ensure that Tang Jingling, Wang Quanzhang, Jiang Tianyong, Wu Gan, Yuan Xinting, and other 709 case lawyers and prisoners of conscience have their basic human rights in prison and make certain that they are not being tortured and are released to reunite with their families.

I hope President Trump can meet with families of the victims in the U.S. before his visit to China, talk about his attention to China's worsening religious freedom and human rights situation during his visit, and give the list of prisoners of conscience to the Embassy.

I believe this is also an important action to maintain universal values all over the world.

Thank you. Wang Yanfang.

[The prepared statement of Ms. Wang follows:]

Subcommittee on Africa, Global Health, Global Human Rights, and International Organizations

U.S. House of Representatives Committee on Foreign Affairs

Disappeared, Jailed and Tortured in China: Wives Petition for Their Husbands' Freedom

Delivered in English by Chia Shih

Rayburn House Office Building Room 2172

Thursday, May 18, 2017

Honorable Chairman Chris Smith, honorable Subcommittee on Africa, Global Health, Global Human Rights, and International Organizations representatives, ladies and gentlemen,

My name is Wang Yanfang, wife of human rights lawyer Tang Jingling. I'd like to express my gratitude to Representative Chris Smith, Senator Marco Rubio, Representative Nancy Pelosi, and many other representatives, as well as Bob Fu, president of ChinaAid Association, for your attention and support of my husband Tang Jingling and many other victims of human rights abuse in China. As the situation of religious freedom, rule of law, and human rights continues to deteriorate in China, support for the victims from the international community is very valuable and precious. This is also an important milestone in joint endeavors to maintain universal values all over the world.

In the past a few decades, people of many countries terminated their seemingly powerful and long-lasting autocratic regimes through non-violent resistance and fulfilled the transition from autocracy to democracy. My husband, Tang Jingling, is a well-known human rights lawyer. He is also the initiator and a keen advocate of the civil disobedience movement. He is dedicated to promoting the civil disobedience movement, hoping to bring forth a democratic and free China.

In 1995, the national security police began to monitor Tang Jingling after he expressed his life-long mission to promote democracy in China. In 1999, he published an article on China's democratization in Guangzhou. Then, he was forced to leave the big law firm he was working for. As a human rights lawyer, he has been involved in many major cases of human rights abuse, political rights abuse, and worker's rights abuse. For example:

In 2003, a petition was initiated to abolish the internment and repatriation regulations and cancel the temporary residence permits policy after college student Sun Zhigang's death. Tang Jingling served as the legal counsel. In 2004, he was the defense lawyer for the two people charged in the Xingang labor unrest case in Dongguan. In January 2005, he defended the newly elected village head in the Shibi third villagers' campaign to remove old village officials. In August 2005, he was one of the key lawyers in the case of the Taishi villagers' campaign to remove village officials. Due to his involvement in human rights cases, the authorities forced his law firm to terminate his employment and suspended his lawyer license. In 2006, he planned to attend an event in the U.S, but he was stopped at customs and his passport was confiscated by the police. He is still not allowed to leave the country to this day.

After losing his lawyer license, he participated in many human rights cases as a citizen, including the poisonous vaccine lawsuit, the investigation of Li Wangyang's death, and many other cases involving land property, forced demolition, and so on.

My husband graduated from Shanghai Jiaotong University in 1993. He began to practice in law in 1998. His lost his lawyer license in 2005 due to his work in human rights protection. During the Jasmine Movement in February 2011, he was charged with "inciting subversion of state power" and was detained in a "black jail," where he was threatened and tortured, including extensive sleep deprivation for 10 days in a row. He was allowed to sleep for 1 to 2 hours a day after he began to have some dangerous symptom, like trembling all over, numbness in both hands, and heart discomfort, until he was released on August 2, 2011.
He initiated and promoted the civil disobedience movement to seek justice for people at the bottom of society, but his wife was forced to lose her job in May 2008. During his detention in February 2011, I was forcibly brought to Conghua and detained. They took my phone, bruised my arms, and didn't allow me to notify my family and lawyer, which caused my severe depression and poor health. Then the police tricked my mother to go to Guangdong to take care of m,e and I was put under house surveillance for a long time. I was not allowed to meet with my family and friends. I was not even allowed to leave my home. More than 20 people took turns watching me. I was completely isolated from the outside world for almost five months. When my husband was released, my physical and mental health had been severely damaged.

On May 16, 2014, Tang Jingling was criminally detained on the charge of "picking quarrels & provoking troubles" and was arrested on June 20 with the charge of "inciting subversion of state power." On September 23, his mother passed away on hearing of his arrest. His lawyer and I applied bail him out to attend his mother's funeral, but the authorities ignored everything on legal, moral, and humanitarian levels and rejected our request. They didn't notify him of her death until October and caused deep sorrow. The authorities forbade his lawyer to meet with him for six months while his case was being transferred to the procuratorate. During the two years in the detention center, all communication was banned. There was no way to guarantee his rights. On January 29, 2016, he was sentenced to five years' imprisonment with the charge of "inciting subversion of state power." He is serving the sentence in Huaiji Prison, Guangdong province.

Since he was arrested in August 2013, I was put under 24-hour surveillance, which brought huge emotional pressure and fear to me. However, I have been appealing for my husband and request that the release him. On July 1, 2014, I went to Hong Kong to attend a demonstration and appealed in the media to urge people to pay attention to Tang Jingling and other prisoners of conscience, like Yuan Chaoyang and Wang Qingying. I was threatened by the police after returning to Guangdong, and my freedom was restricted during the so-called "sensitive" period.

After the massive arrest of human rights lawyers on July 9, 2015, I got in touch with families of arrested human rights lawyers and went to the Supreme People's Procuratorate with them. In August, I was not allowed to leave home.

Since Tang Jingling worked as a lawyer more than a decade ago, he participated in many human rights cases and promoted civil disobedience movement. Consequently, he lost his lawyer license, he was detained, monitored, arrested, tortured, and sentenced, and his wife lost her job, was harassed, summoned, monitored, and detained.

Today other 709 case lawyers are still suffering from such torture. Many prisoners of conscience are still unable to meet with their lawyers and families. Christian churches and still being shut down. Christians are still being detained and sentenced.

Thus, I sincerely plead with President Trump and U.S Congress to urge the Chinese government to guarantee Tang Jingling's right to meet with his lawyer and his rights to reading, communication, medical treatment and food with enough nutrition as well as ensure that Tang Jingling, Wang Quanzhang, Jiang Tianyong, Wu Gan, Yuan Xinting, and the other 709 case lawyers and prisoners of conscience have their basic human rights in prison, and make certain that they are not being tortured and are released to reunite with their families. I hope President Trump can meet with family of the victims in the U.S before his visit to China, talk about his attention to China's worsening religious freedom and human rights situation during his visit, and give the list of prisoners of conscience to the embassy. I believe this is also an important action to maintain universal values all over the world.

Many thanks,

Wang Yanfang

[*Editor's note: The following is a letter written by Tang Jingling while in prison, in which describes his experiences with the Communist government. It was originally published and translated by China Change.*]

A Prisoner's Human Rights Report

"I can't help but sigh over how much more civilized the South African apartheid regime of 50 years ago was compared to the Chinese Communist regime of today." – Tang Jingling

"Other people don't know better than the Chinese people about the human rights condition in China and it is the Chinese people who are in the best situation, in the best position to have a say about China's human rights situation." – Wang Yi, China's Minister of Foreign Affairs, June 2, 2016.

Recalling his nearly 30 years in prison, Nelson Mandela wrote in his memoir *Long Walk to Freedom*: "It is said that no one truly knows a nation until one has been inside its jails. A nation should not be judged by how it treats its highest citizens, but its lowest ones—and South Africa treated its imprisoned African citizens like animals." Having now spent 22 months in Chinese Communist prisons, I'd say that, based on what I've witnessed and experienced, the Chinese Communist Party treats prisoners who don't enjoy special privileges even worse than animals.

And those who are imprisoned for seeking their political rights or defending freedom of religion and other human rights are repressed with particular brutality.

Based on my observations, my impression is that the different levels and standards of prisoner treatment reflect the bureaucratic hierarchy of the country. People who have risen to higher levels of the bureaucracy will be held in a better detention facility or cell or will otherwise receive better treatment. Then there's the principle that originated with the Empress Dowager Cixi: "Better it go to the foreigners than to my slaves." Generally speaking, in other words, foreigners are less likely to be compelled to engage in forced labor, and their religious beliefs are granted a certain degree of respect.

And then there's a large group of prisoners who try to curry favor and build "connections" with people inside the prison in order to enjoy all sorts of special treatment and largess. This leads to an abundance of unfathomable corruption and shady deals. The subjective arbitrariness of prison regulations, the excessive deprivation of prisoners' rights, and the lack of transparency and external oversight have all contributed to this sort of abnormal economy of cash and power within China's notorious system of detention.

Of course, these different classes of treatment are relative among prisoners themselves. On the whole, all prisoners are living under inhumane conditions. It's like one detainee said after being transferred from Guangdong Provincial Detention Center (which mainly holds high-ranked officials) to Baiyun District Detention Center (BDDC): "The moment I stepped foot into the Provincial Detention Center, it was like I'd fallen from high up in the heavens into the depths of hell. I never imagined until I got here that there was an even deeper level of hell!"

The ugliness that exists outside detention facilities is often hidden behind various veils. But inside the wall of the detention center, that ugliness reveals itself unadorned, 24 hours a day. In conditions unfit even for animals, a person must be extremely disciplined to avoid being overcome by hatred and maintain his humanity to avoid being swallowed up by wild beasts. It truly is a very difficult challenge. When it's impossible for us to eliminate evils directly, we must not condone these evils with our silence. Even though I now find myself behind bars because of my efforts on behalf of human rights and democracy, I too am unable to remain silent. For me, this report is my attempt to bear witness to injustice and evil so that I can avoid taking any part in such evils myself.

Below, I will describe seven different aspects of the evil in China's detention centers.

I. Inhumane and degrading treatment, including rampant beatings and torture

On the day I arrived at BDDC, I was kicked by one of the center's auxiliary police officers for refusing to squat down when he ordered me to do so. Within the jail's heavily guarded walls, detainees still wear manacles and shackles around the ankles. When guards escort a detainee from place to place, they often order him to squat as a completely unnecessary way of degrading him. When I got to Guangzhou No. 1 Detention Center, I saw this kind of thing much less frequently, but there were still quite a few prisoners who were treated this way.

I have never seen guards beat any detainees at Guangzhou No. 1, but beatings were not at all uncommon at BDDC. As the guards patrolled the cell block, they would call a detainee to come out of his cell into the passageway. (According to veteran detainees, there weren't enough security cameras to monitor the passageway fully.) First, he would be subjected to a stream of verbal abuse. That was followed by the sound of blows raining down on his body before the injured detainee was returned to his cell. I saw this kind of thing with my own eyes.

At Guangzhou No. 1, I've seen only one detainee—a Uyghur—beaten up like this, and it seemed like that was a common occurrence for Uyghurs like him. Even though the beatings were being carried out by investigators, rather than detention center guards, authorities at the jail and the procuratorial official stationed at the center never made any factual record of those detainees' injuries, let alone file any reports or hold anyone accountable. Han Chinese detainees were no different: the detention center allowed investigators to interrogate detainees for 24 hours straight, with no breaks, until they were finally able to force out the confessions they were looking for.

There was one detainee who entered Guangzhou No. 1 the same month as I did who was interrogated continuously like this for nearly a month and only allowed back in his cell for a short time every day around nightfall. This is a technique commonly used by Communist Party discipline inspectors, and many "official detainees" experience this kind of thing as well. It's just that for them it happens in the illegal private jails set up by the Party's committees for disciplinary inspection. After those "official detainees" offer up their forced confessions there, they get sent to the detention center.

In the cells, each of the cement slabs on which we sleep is fitted with two fixed iron rings. These "fixed shackles" are used by the detention center as a means of disciplinary punishment. A person forced to wear ordinary shackles is still able to move about on his own and take care of many of his daily needs. But once fettered to these fixed shackles, routine daily tasks like eating, getting dressed, or using the toilet all mean that the detainee has to rely on others for everything, making it a terribly agonizing experience.

There's an even more "advanced" and perverse technique, which is to shackle a detainee's hands to the fixed iron rings as well. In this way, even sleep requires one to curl up like some poor shrimp. This type of punishment generally lasts anywhere from a few days to a couple of weeks. In 2014, I saw this in action in Cell 1309. There was a young man clearly suffering from psychological illness and intellectual impairment. The Communist judicial authorities diagnosed him with anti-social personality disorder and sentenced him to 10 years in prison. Because he couldn't control his actions, he was shackled for around a week.

Anyone sentenced to death, regardless of whether or not there's any cause for disciplinary punishment, will also be given the fixed shackles up until the time when he is sent to be executed. One Pakistani man entered the detention center in 2009 and has been subjected to fixed shackling since 2014. Under this long period of suffering, he was forced to write several letters to the Guangdong High Court and the Supreme People's Court begging either to be unshackled or put to death. Wang Qingying (王清莒), who was detained along with me, was given the fixed shackles a number of times and suffered even more serious tortures as well.

I don't know how much longer this kind of inhumane torture will be allowed to continue. Scenes like this serve as a metaphor for the lives of our enslaved people. So much of our agonizing struggles are attempts to break free of these shackles of our bondage. Despite all of their efforts, our people continue to suffer deprivations because those efforts are focused on digging themselves out of the pit associated with their enslavement. Does our generation plan to sit still and remain as slaves, destined to be forgotten by history while the dictatorship flourishes? Or will we make a place for ourselves in history by parting the Red Sea and walking that path out of the desert and into the land of freedom?

An even more common form of inhumane treatment is the overcrowded and confined nature of the cells. Out in the real world, even pigs raised for slaughter aren't treated like this because everyone knows that this will cause serious harm to the pigs. But for months, even years at a time, prisoners are locked up together in these dark, damp, and cramped spaces with no sunlight or fresh air. This in itself causes suffering and is the root of many human rights and humanitarian problems in the detention centers.

For example, it's normal at BDDC to lock up 20 or even 30 people in a space of 20–30 m². The detention center often has a large number of empty cells, so I don't understand why they need to fill cells beyond their capacity like this. Much of the work burden for guards is already being handled by detainee labor and hired security guards, so adding more cells shouldn't be all that difficult.

At BDDC, detainees are typically forced to sleep lying packed together, with one person's feet next to another person's head and vice versa. It's common to be awoken from a deep sleep with a kick in the face from the person next to you or even find your cellmate's toes rubbing up against your mouth. At Guangzhou No. 1 Detention Center, we have to sleep all the way from the cell entrance to right in front of the toilet. The irony is that one of the lines of the detention center rules we were forced to recite every day went like this: "It's forbidden for two people to share a quilt." These days, the authorities make detainees sleep crowded together far more tightly than two people sharing a quilt.

I had another experience that was even more revolting. When I arrived at BDDC they weren't issuing toothbrushes or cups and didn't allow detainees to bring or buy their own. Instead, they forced detainees to use old, discarded toothbrushes and cups and share these among several individuals at once, without any consideration of the fact that many detainees suffered from infectious diseases. Veteran detainees told me that this was not the first time something like this had happened. Fortunately, a clever cellmate of mine fashioned a cup for me out of an old chrysanthemum tea container, which I used until I left that facility. At BDDC, meal trays and spoons were also shared. Guangzhou No. 1 is a bit better in this respect, as each detainee is issued a set of personal items to use upon arrival.

A detainee who had once been jailed in the Tianhe Detention Center told me that detainees there were forced to sit and "meditate" for long periods at a time. I don't know what the situation is like there now, but BDDC had a rule that detainees were required to "meditate" while the guards were patrolling the cell blocks, about a half-hour each morning and each afternoon. The situation is basically the same at Guangzhou No. 1.

II. Forced labor

My labor assignment here consists of keeping watch on the night shift and some manual piece work. Two inmates in each cell are made to keep watch at night. (Sometimes, even more are assigned to this work—especially when conditions are so crowded that there's not enough room to sleep. In Guangdong Provincial Detention Center and other jails where there are fewer prisoners, they don't have this kind of work assignment.) Each shift is made up of two people, who take turns keeping watch for periods of 90 minutes to two hours. Detainees enjoying special treatment don't have to keep watch or do piece work; instead, they get lighter assignments. In some prisons, they have a small number of inmates who are permanently assigned to the night watch, instead of forcing the majority of detainees to be awakened from deep sleep like they do in the detention centers. I think this is a completely unreasonable measure they use to make detainees' lives miserable.

As for manual piece work, there's assembling "red envelopes" and auspicious decorations for Chinese New Year; folding and packing Christmas cards under the brand names "Giftmaker" and "Sue Ryder" (a charity registered in the UK); packing disposable food-service gloves and plastic medical gowns; and affixing advertising stickers for Uni-President Food brands (*a Taiwanese company*). From what I can see, these jobs are pretty steady, so the detention center must have long-term commercial contracts. Rarely has the piece work that I've had to carry out lasted longer than three hours at a time. At BDDC, there wasn't ever any piece work assigned to my cell. But there are cartloads of stuff coming and going in the passageways outside all the time. At Guangzhou No. 1 I have a cellmate from Chongqing who was arrested together with his wife. When they were able to see each other at trial, she told him that the women's cell block had been given very heavy labor assignments and were even forced to work overtime every day late into the evening.

From what I've seen and experienced first-hand, it seems that labor assignments at detention centers have been decreasing but that not much has changed inside the prisons. Outside the VIP cells holding high officials and foreigners, other prisoners still have to work pretty hard. They generally are engaged in rather intensive industrial labor. In this respect, the Ministry of Public Security and Ministry of Justice are actually operating China's biggest sweatshop factories. The millions of detainees they have under their jurisdiction far outnumber the employees of any company in the world.

III. Correspondence, Visits, Meetings, Money, and Goods

In the two years I've been detained, the only time I've been allowed to write a letter was an order form for two books that I sent my wife in March of this year. My lawyer told me that people concerned about me on the outside had been sending me letters and cards, but detention center authorities have been quietly confiscating them all and I haven't seen the slightest trace of any mail. They use these despicable methods against political prisoners in particular. When Mandela was in prison, he was still able to receive letters after they'd first been inspected and censored by the prison authorities. I can't help but sigh over how much more civilized the South African apartheid regime of 50 years ago was compared to the Chinese Communist regime of today. The Chinese authorities inspect all mail and guards can restrict access to letters almost at will, without any rational or predictable rules.

According to the provisions of the *Prison Law*, convicted prisoners may regularly receive visits from family members.* The overwhelming majority of those held in detention centers have not yet been convicted, but without exception they have been deprived of the right to visit with family or friends. Even telephone calls are forbidden! Since many cases drag on for some time without decision, these detainees are completely cut off from their friends and family. The cruelty of this is hard for someone who hasn't experienced it to comprehend. Another side-effect of this inhumane treatment is that it prevents any information from inside the detention center from reaching the outside world, giving the green light to all sorts of corrupt misdeeds and cruel abuse. Ordinary prisoners may keep up with how their family is doing through letters and photographs, but even this is denied political prisoners.

Moreover, the facilities that detention centers make available for meetings with lawyers are often seriously inadequate, and those for visits with family are even worse. Meetings with lawyers are carried out under the eyes and ears of detention center guards, something that people in normal countries with rule of law would probably find unbelievable. Not long after I and other political prisoners arrived at Guangzhou No. 1, the authorities there made a point of "re-arranging" the lawyer meeting room by moving the fixed round-backed chair on which we detainees sit further away from the the dividing screen, which prevents lawyers from showing clients the prosecution files or verifying evidence.

For those detainees who've used their "connections," deliveries of money and "care packages" become a kind of paradise. They have many opportunities to eat food that's been sent in by their families, something that ordinary detainees can only look at with envy. Some of the kinder of these privileged detainees will share their food with their cellmates. These are without doubt the easiest moments to remember in the hellish environment.

Editors' note: Tang's wife recently filed a complaint about being deprived of the right to visit her husband.

IV. Indifference to or outright deprivation of religious freedom

The authorities prohibit religious books that are important to me as a Christian, like the Bible, from being sent into the detention center. Quite a few foreign detainees who are Muslim or Christian can receive copies of the Quran, the Bible, or other religious books in their own languages. But I haven't seen any Uyghur detainees with their own copies of the Quran.

Uyghur detainees are routinely deprived of their religious rights, and though Falun Gong practitioners are deliberately being kept away from where I'm being held, I can't imagine that their situation is any better than mine. Even when their cases aren't connected in any way, political prisoners are deliberately kept apart from each other. Perhaps the Communist authorities learned some lessons from the way that the apartheid government in South Africa imprisoned all of its political prisoners together in one place.

Cultural and educational rights aren't protected either. Not only does the detention center not have a library or reading room, they also prevent detainees from receiving books or subscribing to newspapers or magazines. Political prisoners always want to do some studying on their own, but they're placed under tighter restrictions than ordinary prisoners. It was over a year after I was jailed that I was first allowed to receive a few books sent by my family, but only books related to law were permitted. I had a young Uyghur man in my section of the detention center teach me the Uyghur alphabet and asked my family to send me a Uyghur-Chinese dictionary to help me study the language further. But those plans never got anywhere because of meddling by the authorities.

For the last several months I've again been inexplicably prevented from receiving books. It was only last March that I was finally able to receive two books. And last month was the first time I was able to send out a letter to my family. I've heard that many political prisoners, like Guo Feixiong (郭飞雄) or Xu Zhiyong (许志永), have had to go on hunger strike in order to fight for their right to read.

The ridiculous thing is that every day the detention center authorities force detainees to recite from memory the center regulations, which are mainly about rules of behavior and rights and obligations. They make you recite these every day, and each person has to pass muster. The more rational thing would be to have the detention center employees be the ones who had to memorize and recite these rules. Once you memorize the regulations, then they make you recite a bunch of old moral education rhymes like *Di Zi Gui* (《弟子规》, Rules for Being a Good Student) and *San Zi Jing* (《三字经》, Three Character Classic). Everything depends on how good or bad the detention center officials or guards are, but they don't take into consideration the real needs of detainees at all.

Even if there is some benefit in reciting these texts, the way they're forced on people leads them to become hated. These are just the same old habits of forced brainwashing that the Chinese Communists have always used. Human nature is as easily twisted as the plum blossoms in Gong Zizhen's famous essay, "The Pavilion for Sick Plum Trees." In order to accommodate these ridiculous regulations, many detainees who haven't even been convicted yet already begin proactively copying and memorizing the prison regulations while they're still in the detention center. I never would have believed it if I hadn't seen it with my own eyes!

V. Food and drink, sanitation and medical treatment, and buying things

During the month I was at BDDC, I lost 5 kg because the food was terrible, the portions were small, and I wasn't allowed to purchase any food to supplement. I'm not a fat person to begin with, so a weight loss of 5 kg is no small thing. They only served two meals at BDDC, one at 11 am and the other at 4 pm. Later, after I revealed through my lawyer that they weren't serving us any breakfast, they again started serving breakfast twice a week—a plain steamed bun one day and the other day a bowl of gruel so thin it should technically be called water. I have no idea whether they continued serving that pitiful breakfast after I left. A veteran detainee at BDDC told me that they'd always served breakfast in the past, and he didn't know why they'd recently become so stingy.

For our main daily meal, they'd serve a few pieces of leafy vegetable (but because leafy vegetables were more expensive, they only served them a few times). Typically we'd get some bean sprouts of inferior quality or one or two slices of winter melon, pumpkin, or carrot with a slice or two of fatty pork or the kind of thin ham sausage that's wrapped in plastic. The rice was yellowish and often smelled of mildew. That was pretty much the entire menu. During afternoon calisthenics, I would often feel dizzy because of poor nutrition.

At Guangzhou No. 1, we basically got double what they served at BDDC and the rice was an ordinary white color. They served breakfast of two cold buns or pineapple buns. Both places served winter melon, pumpkin, and white radish with the skin and roots still intact, and they never picked out the yellowed leaves or tough roots of leafy vegetables. At Guangzhou No. 1 for quite a while they gave us frozen duck wings with down still on them that sometimes emitted a terrible odor. According to a jailmate who had worked in the frozen food industry, these likely had been frozen for quite a long time. They were finally removed from the menu only after causing a widespread bout of diarrhea.

Owing to the crowded and confined conditions of detention, sanitation is quite inhumane. Each cell only has a squat toilet, and the water faucet for flushing the toilet is the same one used to get water needed for other daily uses. So when you need to wash bowls and eating utensils, you have to do it right above the toilet. Before they collect the trays after our meals, we have to rinse them very quickly above the toilet before handing them in. Heaven only knows whether or not they wash them again or disinfect them back in the kitchen!

At BDDC, they forced detainees to eat each meal in 3–5 minutes. At Guangzhou No. 1, you get about 10 minutes. According to a detainee who'd been held at the Guangdong Provincial Detention Center, there they have a dedicated washbasin and faucet, separate from the toilet. That proves beyond a doubt that those who operate and manage detention facilities are in fact cognizant of ordinary human needs.

How to dry clothing is also a major problem. There is a row of plastic hooks on the wall of the enclosed courtyard space that's attached to each cell. This is where we're supposed to hang our clothes to dry. The door to this courtyard is only opened once in the morning and once in the afternoon, for less than an hour each time. Sometimes it's even less, not even half an hour. If the weather is rainy, it can take several days for clothes to dry and you have no other clothing to change into. You have no choice but to wear clothes that have grown mildewed from the damp and humidity.

Under these conditions, it's obviously impossible to air out bedding. When one detainee leaves, the bedding he leaves behind will get assigned to a new arrival. Many quilts never lose their musty and mildewed odor. I've heard of some detention facilities where they only close the door to the outside courtyard at night, which is a slightly more humane way of doing things. When I got to Guangzhou No. 1, for some unknown reason the officer who admitted me made a point of giving me the filthiest and most ratty quilt available. Later, I got a newer one from a detainee who was on his way out, and I'm still using that today.

At Guangzhou No. 1, twice a day (excluding holidays) a nurse will distribute medication to detainees who are sick or who suffer from chronic illnesses. Each year, BDDC holds more than 5,000 detainees—several times more than Guangzhou No. 1. During the month I was at BDDC, I never saw any medical care like we have here.

When I got to the detention center, I increased my physical exercise and I could clearly feel my health improving a bit. But I catch colds far more frequently here than I did on the outside. I think that's obviously a result of the terrible sanitary conditions and nutrition here. We have to bathe with cold water, even in the fall and winter, which is another reason many people get sick.

Generally, the 500 yuan each person can spend each month to purchase items goes to the purchase of daily items (underwear and a limited selection of supplementary foods). This is based on a provision in the Detention Center Regulations that was set many years ago (in 1990). If the food provided by the detention centers didn't leave detainees feeling hungry, this monthly amount would be sufficient even with today's prices. Goods are typically bought in group purchases twice a month, with detainees using an order form provided by the detention center to mark down what they want and the desired quantities. I've also heard of detention centers where they offer detainees a variety of meals, turning the jail into a kind of restaurant and general store.

Luckily, I've never been sick enough to require being hospitalized. Based on what I've heard from others who have, the detainee wing at the Guangzhou People's Armed Police (PAP) Hospital has earned the nickname "Police Beatings Hospital." What sick people need is treatment and care, but most people's memory of that place is that it's even worse than jail itself. Patients are assigned only one set of clothes, and if they want to launder them they have go around naked in the meantime. Patients wear leg shackles the whole time, and quite often some will get shackled to their beds because of some trivial matter and left lying in their own excrement while no one bothers with them.

Security guards beat patients for no reason, and the food is no better than in the detention centers. In the case of Guangzhou No. 1, the food is probably even worse and they don't allow patients to buy extra food while in the hospital. The medical staff is very curt and brutish. One cellmate I had spent nearly a year in the hospital, off and on, and witnessed many cases of gauze being left in patients' bodies after an operation. It got to the point where he finally became afraid to admit that he was sick for fear of being sent to the PAP Hospital. It's said that ill detainees from detention centers all over the province get sent there and that there are more than 500 people being held in the detainee wing.

VI. Disciplinary measures, relief procedures, and sham oversight provisions

Even though the prison uses fixed shackling and other brutal disciplinary measures to punish detainees, I've never seen the detention facility carry out any legal procedure in connection with this.

When the officers take such measures, detainees have no chance to defend themselves. What the officers are acting out here is a real-life legal farce. On the surface, the resident procuratorate office is supposed to carry out oversight of the detention centers, but in the two years I've been in detention I've only seen a single detainee have a meeting with a resident procuratorate official on official business. I've never seen anything in writing about how to contact the procuratorate. How can he carry out his duties of oversight of the legal system and protection of human rights?

VII. Detainees with special privileges

In February of this year, as I was being transferred from Cell Unit 5 to Cell Unit 3, I discovered that a single person was being held all by himself in Cell No. 1301. That man (who people said was a former vice governor of Hainan Province) was clearly living in a newly renovated cell that was just like a hotel. He enjoyed quite a few different kinds of special treatment. His cell was kept open for long periods at a time to prevent him from feeling as if he were being held in a confined space. (It was precisely for this reason that we were able to see a bit of the conditions under which he was being held.) They say he receives the same meals that the guards do.

Cell No. 1302, right next door, is also a special-treatment cell where a dozen or so men are held under much lower security. According to other detainees with good sources of information, those detainees also enjoy much better food than ordinary prisoners—each of them might get a raw cucumber or an extra egg each day. Privileged detainees like these are able to enjoy a standard of living far superior to that offered to ordinary prisoners. This is a microcosm of the same distribution gap that exists between ordinary people and the privileged Communist Party elite outside prison.

Many detainees rely on cultivating "connections" to improve their treatment. They'll get new bedding and clothing. They'll be given drier and more airy places to sleep. They won't have to take overnight shifts or do manual piece work. Instead they'll get light tasks to do or oversee the piece work done by other detainees. Some are even given the job of assigning daily chores among the other detainees, or what is known as being the "jail boss."

It's the detention center officers who hand out these assignments. I once heard of a person who spent several thousand yuan each month in an unsuccessful attempt to bribe the guards to give him the position of "jail boss." Whether ordinary prisoners are treated with basic humanity depends entirely on personal favors from a few detention center guards. As long as the authorities continue to closely monitor and restrict detainees from meeting or corresponding with relatives and lawyers, then it's wishful thinking for them to harbor any hopes of wiping out this kind of corruption.

I haven't yet been transferred to prison, where individuals who've already been convicted are incarcerated. So, I don't have much to say here about conditions in China's prisons. But based on the many cases about which I've seen and heard, there are many similarities between prisons and detention centers.

Some might think that what I've reported here is based solely on my own personal experience and decide that it's not a representative enough sample. What I've discussed here is mainly based on my personal experience, but for the past two years I've been lived 24 hours a day with a total of over 200 other detainees of all types. Many among them have spent time in other detention centers and prisons at different times and in different places. Of what they've told me, I've only included details that I have been able to corroborate.

I don't expect the Communist authorities to undertake any reform as a result of this report, but I hope that I myself won't become numb to these re-occurring atrocities and sink into a kind of degradation. For me, then, this is a way to seek my own salvation.

All men and women of the world who are willing to speak out for justice and humanity: Please listen to what I've said here and speak up on behalf of those of us who have already lost our ability to speak for ourselves. I pray that you will be blessed by God's righteousness!

Tang Jingling

April 26, 2016

Mr. SMITH. Thank you so very much for your very moving statement.

And I would like to now yield such time as you may consume to Ms. Jin.

STATEMENT OF MS. JIN BIANLING, SPOUSE OF JIANG TIANYONG

[The following statement and answers were delivered through an interpreter.]

Ms. JIN. Honorable Chairman Chris Smith, Honorable Subcommittee on Africa, Global Health, Global Human Rights, and International Organizations Representatives, ladies and gentlemen, thank you very much for your attention to my husband Jiang Tianyong's suffering.

Jiang Tianyong is a Chinese human rights lawyer. He began to advocate for human rights in 2006, representing hepatitis B patients, AIDS patients, and numerous Falun Gong practitioners.

In order to promote the legal rights of lawyers, he contributed to the direct election of the Beijing Lawyers Association and exposed corruptions within the Beijing judicial system, such as blackmailing and racketeering. I am willing to provide photographic evidence of our heavy surveillance surrounding our house in China and also the audio recording of my husband when he was disappeared during the Jasmine Revolution.

On October 29, 2009, Jiang Tianyong participated in a U.S. congressional hearing and spoke on the main theme, which was the problem with China's legal system and religion.

I am bearing witness to how the national security police retaliated against our entire family as a result of this testimony.

Ever since Tianyong was forced to stay home on sensitive dates, such as meetings of the National People's Congress, the Political Consultative Conference, June 4, which is the anniversary of the 1989 Tiananmen Square Massacre, or during important political leaders' visits to China, he could only get out of the house by taking their police cars. I have videos to verify all of this.

Beginning on February 15, 2011, Tianyong disappeared for 2 months during the Jasmine Revolution. He was brutally beaten, deprived of sleep, forced to watch CCTV news, sing songs, and recite patriotic articles to praise the Chinese Communist Government, and write thousands of pages of repentance letters. The videos can serve as evidence.

On May 3, 2012, five national security agents from the Haidian District, Beijing, represented by Du Yuhui, beat Tianyong up when he attempted to visit the barefoot lawyer, Chen Guangcheng, at the hospital. Tianyong temporarily lost his hearing due to the perforation of his left ear's tympanic membrane. The police repeatedly took Tianyong away for questioning and threatened him, saying that our child could not go to school if he refused to cooperate. They also said that I, as his wife, could be affected as well. The long-term harassment and threats consumed me.

I even thought of suicide. My child's mental condition was severely disrupted. Desperate, I brought my daughter to the U.S. in May 2013.

On March 20, 2014, the local national security agents arrested Tianyong again in Jiansanjiang, Heilongjiang while he was representing Falun Gong practitioners. The police broke eight of Tianyong's ribs during the 16 days of detention. I have the diagnosis from the hospital as proof.

On November 21, 2016, Jiang Tianyong disappeared on his way back to Beijing after visiting the family members of lawyer Xie Yang. Now the government has already banned him from meeting with lawyers for 178 days and we do not know where he is detained. Tianyong's parents have been put under surveillance. The national security agents follow them wherever they go. According to the news on May 12, 2017, Tianyong has been tortured, and his legs are too swollen to walk.

In order to safeguard human rights and the universal worth of defending legal rights, I strongly hope the Honorable President Trump and the U.S. Congress can immediately and effective urge China's central Government to investigate the actual facts behind the torture of those arrested in the 709 crackdown, simultaneously enacting legal sanctions against those who practice torture and request that China clearly ensures that other incarcerated prisoners of conscience do not continue to receive harm.

In addition, I want to mention that Tianyong has already received a letter confirming his political asylum in the United States. I hope that President Trump can negotiate with the Chinese Government during his visit and let Tianyong reunite with me and my daughter.

May 19th is Tianyong's 46th birthday. I hereby make a wish on behalf of Tianyong and our family. I hope he can regain freedom so his aging parents would not have to worry constantly and his daughter could have her wish fulfilled and embrace her father.

I hope I can forever set aside my heart, which anxiously worries about Tianyong, and a tranquil and merry life can come to our household.

Thank you. Jin Bianling.

[The prepared statement of Ms. Jin follows:]

Subcommittee on Africa, Global Health, Global Human Rights, and International Organizations

U.S. House of Representatives Committee on Foreign Affairs

Disappeared, Jailed and Tortured in China: Wives Petition for Their Husbands' Freedom

Testimony of Jin Bianling Delivered in English by Mino Shih

Rayburn House Office Building Room 2172

Thursday, May 18, 2017

Honorable Chairman Chris Smith, honorable Subcommittee on Africa, Global Health, Global Human Rights, and International Organizations representatives, ladies and gentlemen,

Thank you very much for your attention to my husband Jiang Tianyong's suffering. The Chinese government forbids its citizens to comment on events concerning human rights; therefore, the support and attention from the international society is crucial to suppressed individuals and groups.

Jiang Tianyong is a Chinese human rights lawyer. He began to advocate for human rights in 2006, representing hepatitis B patients, AIDS patients, and numerous Falun Gong practitioners. In order to promote the legal rights of lawyers, he contributed to the direct election of the Beijing Lawyers' Association and exposed corruptions within the Beijing judicial system, such as blackmailing and racketeering. Jiang Tianyong is willing to take all kinds of risks to represent the weak and improve human rights conditions in China.

On Oct. 29, 2009, Jiang Tianyong participated in a U.S. Congressional hearing and spoke on the main theme, which was "The Problem with China's Legal System and Religion." This time, I am bearing witness to how the national security police retaliated against our entire family. From November 17-18, 2009, former President Obama visited China. It was a sensitive period for the Chinese Communist government, because the officials feared that the human right activists would get in contact with Mr. Obama. Jiang Tianyong was therefore put under house arrest. Our child was in first grade at the time. We all thought that Tianyong could regain freedom once Mr. Obama returned to the United States. On the morning of Nov. 19, 2009, four police officials in casual clothes grabbed Tianyong and threw him to the ground when he accompanied our child to school. My child was so scared that she began to cry out loud. National security policeman Wang Tao also pushed me to the ground when I arrived at the scene. The police detained Tianyong at the Yangfangdian Police Station in Haidian District, Beijing for 13 hours. During the evening, my child told me after school that two national security police officials went to her school on that day, asked her about what had happened in the morning without the consent of her guardians, filed the conversation, and asked her to sign the record. Tianyong was detained for 13 hours and released after he had reached an agreement with policeman Wang Tao. The agreement between Jiang Tianyong and Wang Tao can testify to the aforementioned event.

Ever since, Tianyong was forced to stay home on "sensitive" dates, such as meetings

[*Editor's note: This is the anniversary of the 1989 Tiananmen Square Massacre*], or during important political leaders' visits to China. He could only get out of the house by taking their police cars. I have videos to verify all of this.

Beginning on Feb. 15, 2011, Tianyong disappeared for two months during the Jasmine Revolution. He was brutally beaten, deprived of sleep, forced to watch CCTV News, sing songs and recite patriotic articles to praise the Chinese Communist Government, and write thousands of pages of repentance letters. The videos can serve as evidence.

On May 3, 2012, five national security agents from Haidian District, Beijing, represented by Du Yuhui, beat Tianyong up when he attempted to visit the barefoot lawyer Chen Guangcheng at the hospital. Tianyong temporarily lost his hearing due to the perforation of his left ear's tympanic membrane, but the police prevented him from going to the doctor. After protesting, Tianyong had his ear checked at the Shijitan Hospital in Beijing, and the doctor claimed that there was nothing wrong with it. A few months later, Tianyong went to a hospital in Zhengzhou, and the doctors there diagnosed him with perforation of the left ear's tympanic membrane. The medical certificate issued by the hospital can prove what I said.

The police repeatedly took Tianyong away for questioning and threatened him, saying that our child could not go to school if he refused to cooperate; they also said that I as his wife could be affected as well. The long-term harassment and threats consumed me. I even thought of suicide. My child's mental condition was severely disrupted. Desperate, I brought my daughter to the U.S. in May 2013.

On March 20, 2014, the local national security agents arrested Tianyong again in Jiansanjiang, Heilongjiang, while he was representing Falun Gong practitioners. The police broke eight of Tianyong's ribs during the 16 days of detention. I have the diagnosis from the hospital as proof. In July 2015, the 709 crackdown occurred. Many lawyers and citizens were arrested. Tianyong was ready to rescue the arrested human right activists; he had to change residences every day in order to hide from the national security agents.

On November 21, 2016, Jiang Tianyong disappeared on his way back to Beijing after visiting the family members of Lawyer Xie Yang. Now, the government has already banned him from meeting with lawyers for 178 days, and we do not know where he is detained. Tianyong's parents have been put under surveillance; the national security agents follow them wherever they go. According to news on May 12, 2017, Tianyong has been tortured, and his legs are too swollen to walk.

In order to safeguard human rights and the universal worth of defending legal rights, I strongly hope the honorable President Trump and the U.S. Congress can immediately and effectively urge China's central government to investigate the actual facts behind the torture of those arrested in the 709 crackdown—simultaneously enacting legal sanctions against those who practiced torture—and request that China clearly ensures that other incarcerated prisoners of conscience do not continue to receive harm. The Global Magnitsky Human Rights Accountability Act sheds some hope into the miserable condition of China, and I hope President Trump helps supervise the enforcement of the Act. Meanwhile, I hope President Trump will meet with the victims' family members before going to China, express his concerns about the deterioration of human rights conditions and the freedom of religion, and publically provide the Chinese government with a list of prisoners of conscience during his visit

In addition, I want to mention that Tianyong has already received a letter confirming his political asylum in the United States. I hope that President Trump can negotiate with the Chinese government during his visit and let Tianyong reunite with me and my daughter.

May 19 BST is Tianyong's 46th birthday. I hereby make a wish on behalf of Tianyong and our family: I hope he can regain freedom, so his aging parents would not have to worry constantly and his daughter could have her wish fulfilled and embrace her father. I hope I can forever set aside my heart, which anxiously worries about Tianyong, and a tranquil and merry life can come to our household.

Thank you

Jin Bianling

———————

Mr. SMITH. Ms. Jin, thank you so very much.

I would like to now yield to Ms. Li.

STATEMENT OF MS. LI CHING-YU, SPOUSE OF LEE MIN-CHE

[The following statement and answers were delivered through an interpreter.]

Ms. LI. Chairman Smith, members of the committee, good afternoon. I am Li Ching-Yu, wife of Li Ming-Che.

I would like to thank each of you for upholding and defending the values of freedom and democracy, values that human rights activists, including my husband, have dedicated their entire lives and energies to. I would also like to express my gratitude toward all the congressmen, especially Chairman Royce and Chairman Smith, who strive to maintain and further secure the implementation of the Taiwan Relations Act.

I am deeply honored to be here today alongside these three respectable women who have gone through such perilous situations for the cause of democracy and human rights.

It's after hearing about their journeys that I realized how fortunate I am as a Taiwanese. I further understood the blessings of our democracy, which exists today, thanks to the support of the U.S. Government and all the 20th century Taiwanese human rights activists, as mentioned by Chairman Royce in the March 14, 2014, hearing on the TRA.

My husband, Li Ming-Che is from a—is from a Chinese refugee family that emigrated to Taiwan following the nationalist government in 1949.

His background and emotional connection to China have contributed to his supports of Chinese human rights efforts. From 2012 until his disappearance, he gave online lectures through WeChat on the democratization of Taiwan and the history of the White Terror period. He also managed and contributed to a social justice fund for the purpose of financially supporting Chinese political prisoners and their families experiencing economic hardship that stemmed from their support of the values of freedom, justice, and democracy.

On March 19, 2017, while on an annual visit to China to meet with people he worked on the fund with, my husband was subjugated to enforced incommunicado detention. It's been 61 days since I last saw him. I am concerned. I am concerned about his health, for he suffers from high blood pressure. I am concerned for his safety. I do not know where he is for the Guangdong government has refused to disclose the location of his detention.

The deprivation of my husband's liberty by the local Guangdong government is arbitrary and transgresses Articles 9, 19, and 20 of the Universal Declaration of Human Rights, the Cross-Strait Joint Crime-Fighting and Judicial Mutual Assistance Agreement, and International Covenant on Civil and Political Rights.

It was not long after my husband's enforced disappearance that I learned about his detainment from a middleman. Since current cross-strait relations are highly abnormal, many such cases that involve Taiwanese people being detained or arrested in China are settled through brokers. These brokers for the most part represent the interests of the PRC. I was shown a copy of a letter that was written under involuntary circumstances by my husband.

This letter was in the hands of Li Jun-min, a representative of the PRC Taiwan Affairs Office. He threatened me, insisting that I cancel my trip to Beijing and also silence myself. Li expressed clearly that the detention originated as a result of the provincial government of Guangdong's desire to show its strict enforcement of the newly-passed foreign NGO management law. He threatened that if I were to go to Beijing, the local Guangdong government would release a video of my husband admitting to having committed criminal actions.

The U.S. has long insisted that its policy of no negotiation with terrorists is to be firmly followed. I also believe in that policy. I refuse to negotiate with a broker on such unequal grounds. If I did, it would be harmful and shameful to my family, my country, and my fellow human rights activists.

Additionally, to my great disappointment, the Chinese Government has unreasonably revoked my travel visa, even though I have clearly and calmly explained that I only wanted to travel to better understand the situation.

China's position toward human rights and the rule of law is drastically different from that of Taiwan and other civilized democratic countries. China should not assume that their military and economic growth could force Taiwan to be annexed by it.

If China maintains that my husband's actions of spreading the values of democracy and aiding the family of members of political prisoners can pose a threat to its national security, I believe the people of Taiwan will become not only more certain of their unwillingness to be annexed but also hesitant to preserve a close relationship with China. It has only been around 20 years since Taiwan successfully overthrew the White Terror's one-party dictatorship. So it is highly unlikely that we will be willing to accept another despotic government.

I have no other choice but to come and stand before you to ask for help from you. United States of America is the leading democracy in the free world. It was built upon the unalienable rights of life, liberty, and the pursuit of happiness.

The U.S. has long been the protector of justice, freedom, and democracy everywhere. It has accepted the moral obligation to aid people deprived of their natural rights. The American Congress' unwavering dedication toward these values has influenced many countries including my home country, Taiwan, to embrace the spirit of human rights and democracy.

The U.S. Congress has also voluntarily taken the responsibility as specified in Section 2, Clause 3 of the Taiwan Relations Act, to preserve and enhance the human rights of the people of Taiwan. Therefore, I stand alone before you today to plea for your help for my husband. I am pleading to the United States to continue to act as according to the TRA. I am pleading the United States to continue to support the value of which it has always unbendingly defended. I am pleading to the United States to continue to uphold the values of which it was formed upon. I am pleading to the U.S. Government to pressure China to recognize the provincial government of Guangdong's illegitimate detention of my husband, Li Ming-Che, and free him.

Thank you. Li Ching-yu.

[The prepared statement of Ms. Li follows:]

Testimony of Li Ching-Yu, delivered in English by Jasmine Chia Shih

Subcommittee Chairman Smith, members of the committee,

Good afternoon,

I am Li Ching-Yu, wife of Li Ming-Che. I would like to thank each of you for upholding and defending the values of freedom and democracy, values that human rights activists, including my husband, have dedicated their entire lives and energies to. I would also like to express my gratitude towards all the congressmen, especially Chairman Royce and Subcommittee Chairman Smith, who strived to maintain and further secure the implementation of the Taiwan Relations Act.

I am deeply honored to be here today, alongside these three respectable women, who have gone through such perilous situations for the cause of democracy and human rights. Your stories are truly inspiring. It is after hearing about their journeys that I realized how fortunate I am, as a Taiwanese. I further understood the blessings of our democracy, which exists today thanks to the support of the U.S. government, and all the 20th Century Taiwanese human rights activists, as mentioned by Chairman Royce in the March 14, 2014 hearing on the TRA.

(The rest of my testimony will be read directly by Ms. Jasmine Chia Shih)

My husband, Li Ming-Che, is from a Chinese refugee family that immigrated to Taiwan following the nationalist government in 1949. His background and emotional connection to China have contributed to his support of Chinese human rights efforts. From

2012 until his disappearance, he gave online lectures through WeChat on the democratization of Taiwan and the history of the White Terror period. He also managed and contributed to a social justice fund for the purpose of financially supporting Chinese political prisoners and their families experiencing economic hardship that stemmed from their support of the values of freedom, justice, and democracy.

On March 19, 2017, while on an annual visit to China to meet with people he worked on the fund with, my husband was subjugated to enforced incommunicado detention. It has been 61 days since I last saw him.

I am concerned. I am concerned about his health for he suffers from high blood pressure. I am concerned for his safety.

I do not know where he is for the Guangdong government has refused to disclose the location of his detention.

The deprivation of my husband's liberty by the local Guangdong government is arbitrary and transgresses the articles 9, 19, and 20 of the Universal Declaration of Human Rights, the Cross-Strait Joint Crime-Fighting and Judicial Mutual Assistance Agreement, and the International Covenant on Civil and Political Rights.

It was not long after my husband's enforced disappearance that I learned about his detainment, from a middle man. Since current cross-strait relations are highly abnormal, many such cases that involve Taiwanese people being detained or arrested in China are settled through brokers. These brokers, for the most part, represent the interests of the PRC.

I was shown a copy of a letter that was written under involuntary circumstances by my husband. This letter was in the hands of Lee Jun-min, a representative of the PRC Taiwan Affairs Office. He threatened me, insisting that I cancel my trip to Beijing and also silence myself. Lee expressed clearly that the detention originated as a result of the provincial government of Guangdong's desire to show its strict enforcement of the newly passed Foreign NGO management law. He threatened that if I were to go to Beijing, the local Guangdong government would release a video of my husband admitting to having committed criminal actions.

The U.S. has long insisted that its policy of no negotiation with terrorists is to be firmly followed. I also believe in that policy. I refused to negotiate with the broker on such unequal grounds. If I did, it would be harmful and shameful to my family, my country, and my fellow human rights activists. Additionally, to my great disappointment, the Chinese government has unreasonably revoked my travel visa, even though I have clearly and calmly explained that I only wanted to travel to better understand the situation.

China's position towards human rights and the rule of law is drastically different from that of Taiwan and other civilized democratic countries. China should not assume that their military and economic growth could force Taiwan to be annexed by it. If China maintains that my husband's actions of spreading the values of democracy and aiding the family members of political prisoners compose a threat to its national security, I believe the people of Taiwan will become not only more certain of their unwillingness to be annexed but also hesitant to preserve a close relationship with China.

It has only been around 20 years since Taiwan successfully overthrew the White Terror's one-party dictatorship. So it is highly unlikely that we will be willing to accept another despotic government.

I have no other choice but to come and stand before you, to ask for help from you. The United States of America is the leading democracy in the free world. It was built upon the unalienable rights of life, liberty, and the pursuit of happiness. The U.S. has long been the protector of justice, freedom, and democracy everywhere. It has accepted the moral obligation to aid people deprived of their natural rights. The American Congress's unwavering dedication towards these values has influenced many countries, including my home country Taiwan, to embrace the spirit of human rights and democracy. The U.S. Congress has also voluntarily taken the responsibility, as specified in section 2, clause 3 of the Taiwan Relations Act, to preserve and enhance the human rights of the people of Taiwan.

Therefore, I stand alone before you today to plea for your help for my husband. I am pleading the United States to continue to act as according to the TRA. I am pleading the United States to continue to support the value of which it has always unbendingly defended. I am pleading the United States to continue to uphold the values of which it was formed upon. I am pleading the U.S. government to pressure China to recognize the provincial government of Guangdong's illegitimate detention of my husband, Li Ming-Che, and free him.

Thank you.

Mr. SMITH. Ms. Li, thank you very much as well for your testimony.

Finally, the Taiwanese Government is working behind the scenes to resolve the case of Li Ming-Che, although I am sure such efforts are hindered by Taiwan's complicated diplomatic ties with Beijing.

As I've said before, Taiwan is an important democratic ally and a beacon of peace and democracy in Asia. The U.S. should remain committed to the Taiwan Relations Act and the Six Assurances as the cornerstone of U.S.-Taiwan relations. Political issues between China and Taiwan should be resolved through appropriate mechanisms between the two sides. The Chinese Government's decision to detain Li Ming-Che singled Chinese officials' willingness to break its international human rights obligations for political gains, again, needlessly straining the cross-strait ties.

We do have a video, about a 4-minute video. It was sent to us by the wives of lawyers of Li Heping and Wang Quanzhang. It features Wang Qiaoling and Li Wenzu and it will now play for us.

[Video shown.]

Thank you so very much for those insights, horrible and brutal as they are, concerning the torture.

Let me ask a few questions and then I will yield to my colleagues for any questions they might have, and first of all, let me begin by saying to Ms. Jin how heartbroken I and others are over your husband's incarceration.

I will remind members of our subcommittee that your husband testified on November 10, 2009, at a hearing that I chaired. He very much wanted to present testimony as a human rights lawyer.

It was the Tom Lantos Commission and I was chairing that hearing, and without objection, his testimony from that hearing will be made a part of this record as well.

But he was very firm, very clear in his testimony. He talked about working with Chen Guangcheng on behalf of women who had been subjected to the brutality of the one-child-per-couple policy—a policy that treats women as chattel and kills their children and does so right up into the 9th month of pregnancy. As we all know, under that brutal policy there are now missing about 62 million females, a direct result of sex-selection abortion, causing huge disparities in the male-female ratio.

But, as you know, Ms. Jin, your husband bravely tried to defend the women from this assault and for that he was incarcerated.

I would add to that that he returned to China—and this underscores something that has to come out of this hearing and all of our efforts going forward. He went back to China. President Obama was in Beijing. He asked and thought he had a meeting with him along with some of the other human rights lawyers. He did not. And hours after the President of the United States left on Air Force One, he was arrested and his horrific ordeal that continues to this day continues.

It shows, in my opinion, that there is a consequence for being so brave, which is why we are all concerned about you and your husbands and the fact that at the highest levels of government, and this appeal is to the President of the United States today and the Vice President, Mike Pence, that our voice has to be clear.

We have to look Xi Jinping and other top leaders in the eye, have names, lists, the way Reagan did, and did so effectively during the worst days of the Soviet Union, when there was always a list of dissidents, human rights activists, and Jewish refuseniks that he would tender to the leaders of the Soviet Union, and those people—not all, but many of them got out and for many others the torture was ameliorated because we paid attention to what was going on. I would also add that we will ask President Trump—we will present him with your testimonies—and Vice President Pence—and ask him to meet with you and I would add we would ask him to meet with the five daughters as well and a few other very notable human rights activists who have suffered for their convictions in China.

We had five daughters here presenting testimony in 2013. We called it the Five Daughters Hearing. They all had a dad who was incarcerated and subjected to torture. We asked President Obama to meet with them so that when he met with Hu Jintao, and after that Xi Jinping, he would have their cases and their pleas, their appeals, often through tears, uppermost in his mind to convey that agony to the leader of the Chinese Government.

We tried for months to arrange that meeting. At the end of about 6 months we were told by the White House he doesn't have the time.

Now, if President Trump and Vice President Pence gives the same indifference, same answer, which I think is a callous disregard for suffering people, I will be here at this podium speaking out against that lack of concern and empathy for suffering people. Those young ladies said at that hearing President Obama has two daughters—he'll understand what it's like for a daughter to speak on behalf of her father. You, as wives, are doing exactly the same and I want you to know we, in this subcommittee, both sides of the aisle, have nothing but concern and empathy for each and every one of you, for your husbands, for your families.

And just a couple of very quick questions. When your husbands are incarcerated, and many of you spoke about this—Ms. Wang, you spoke of being severely damaged physically and mentally because of your husband's incarceration. The Chinese dictatorship knows that when they arrest your husbands or any dissident or prisoner of conscience the whole family goes to jail.

They know that the friends of the family of the incarcerated individual goes to jail as well. All the more reason why we need to significantly up our voices, make our voices much clearer in Congress and at the White House, at the State Department, and added to that, we need to use the tools that are at our disposal from Country of Particular Concern for religious believers, sanctioning the Government of China for its egregious human rights violations on religious freedom, use the Trafficking Victims Protection Act and make them a Tier 3 country, which they deserve to be for the government's complicity in human trafficking which is bad and getting worse.

And then for the political dissidents like your husbands, who represent a cross-section of suffering individuals in China, including labor rights. There is no doubt that China does not respect ILO standards—International Labour Organization standards—from collective bargaining to even paying a decent wage, and with impunity they crush independent trade union efforts. We have had at our hearings in the past leaders of that movement come and testify and say, yes, they have a labor union run by the government—it is a farce.

So my question would be the impact on the families and also, if you would, speak to your hopes and expectations of what we might do next.

Again, I think you've said it in your testimonies—implement our laws. We have a toolbox filled with the capacity to hold China to account. Magnitsky is just the latest iteration of a tool that can't stay in that toolbox. And the Chinese Government must know, collectively as a government and individually, those who commit these crimes need to be held to account and we have the tools to do it.

So yes, Ms. Chen.

Ms. CHEN. I have the latest news today. Those public security officers threatened my husband and the family members that if I do not return to China, they will give him a heavier sentence. So I feel, even in the United States, I don't feel safe, and I am haunted, and I really seek protection by the U.S.

Mr. SMITH. Would anybody else like to comment before I yield to Mr. Castro? Yes.

Ms. CHEN. So I call upon the U.S. Government to express to the Chinese Government to stop the—this kind of brutal persecution against the victims of the 709 cases and their family members and to restore their dignity. Because the Chinese Government is also a signatory country of the anti-torture international covenant. So I want to call upon the Chinese Government to release the videos of during these victims' incarceration and to show what they have gone through.

And because all the family members of the 709 cases and others persecuted, their children are stopped by the Chinese Government for education and schooling, and President Trump has his own children, so I do hope he can meet with ours. We can express that to him face to face, and also our family members inside China.

Mr. SMITH. Ms. Jin.

Ms. JIN. By June 1st, it is already 6 months of my husband, Jiang Tianyong's, enforced disappearance. Right now, both of his parents are being monitored and followed closely. They were forced to write promises that they would not communicate or have any contact with me. Of course, we just heard from Ms. Wang Qiaoling, the wife of Li Heping, who revealed the torture he had experienced. Jiang Tianyong also had been experiencing torture.

And the similar experience of being drugged was also shared by other recently released human rights lawyers, like Li Chunfu, like Li Shuyun, and, of course, Li Heping. And to the point attorney Li Chunfu was even tortured with serious mental illness.

Even last night, the Chinese official microblog, Weibo, showed a short video clip. On that video, it shows my husband, Jiang Tianyong, was kind of walking, and on that video, it claims that Jiang Tianyong was not tortured. But when I observed that short video, I noticed on the legs, both legs of Jiang Tianyong the kind of black and blue marks are still there on his legs, and his face has been very swollen and his right arm cannot move when he walked.

So I could not believe what the government claimed, that he was not tortured. So I am deeply concerned about what's happening with Jiang Tianyong and his well-being and his life, and even until today he was denied lawyer's visitation. And further, Jiang Tianyong has already been approved as a U.S. asylee, granted by the U.S. Government in 2016 already. But the Chinese regime refused to let him exit from China. I hope President Trump can really express this point with the Chinese leaders and plead with the Chinese Government release Jiang Tianyong and to have family reunion here in the United States with us.

Today is Jiang Tianyong's birthday. My daughter and I have been here for 4 years but we have never met again. My daughter is really, really eager to hug her daddy.

Mr. SMITH. Thank you.

Mr. Castro.

Mr. CASTRO. I think they just called votes and so I want to say thank you to each of you for your courage and your bravery in coming here to Congress and telling us your stories.

I hope that you'll continue to give us counsel and guidance on how you believe the United States can be more helpful as it comes to China and the issue of human rights and we, in turn, will mon- itor not only your situations and the situations of your husbands but also of others who are going through similar things in China. And as I mentioned earlier, this should be an effort not only for the United States but also for the allies of the United States around the world.

So your suggestions on how you believe that the friends of the United States, those nations who also believe in strong human rights can be helpful with respect to China and ensuring that China is a place that respects the human rights of its people and the freedoms of its people. Thank you for being here.

Mr. SMITH. Mr. Castro, thank you very much.

Mr. Garrett.

Mr. GARRETT. Thank you, Mr. Chairman.

It's troubling as I review the remarks of the ladies here today and consider that not only were the victims of the 709 crackdown jailed and subsequently tortured because they were brave enough to take a stand in favor of human rights but that in fact it would appear that a meeting planned with the United States President may have been a pretext for an arrest of other individuals in China.

As a member of this subcommittee, I understand that when we hold hearings such as this it is our responsibility to try to work to help people. But it is my fear that your courage in being here might be used as a pretext again to hurt people.

With that said, I understand that as one Member of 435 and one of two chambers in a legislative body there is only so much that I can do. But I want to be abundantly clear for the record and for these brave women. To the extent that I have the ability to cast a vote that will deal favorably or unfavorably with the regime based on how it treats its own citizens and people who seek to affect positive human rights changes, I will consider their actions when I make my vote.

To the extent that I have the ability to put forward policy that will shape the United States policy as it relates to nations based on how they treat their citizens and other citizens, I will consider these things in how I advance policy.

And to the extent I am able to influence my colleagues and the executive branch of this government as it relates to relations with foreign nations to include dominant global forces such as the People's Republic of China, I will consider how they treat their people and other people as it relates to human rights when I seek to exert that influence.

We shouldn't convene committee hearings to help people that we know have the potential to lead to greater harm to people without ensuring the folks that we seek to help, you all, that we will do everything in our power to make sure that all we can effect that is good is affected.

With that, I offer my admiration and my thanks for the courage of these ladies, my encouragement for people who, in China as everywhere, seek basic human rights as outlined in foundational American documents—life, liberty, and the pursuit of happiness—but as aspired to by people across the globe and promise that within my small ability to make a difference I will side with human rights and with people who have suffered like yourselves wherever possible and I appreciate the chairman for creating this opportunity and I commend your courage, and to the extent it is appropriate you have my prayers and my promise to do what I can.

Mr. SMITH. Mr. Garrett, thank you very much for that very strong statement. And you are right, they all have our prayers as well as everything we can do as a committee in a bipartisan way and as a Congress to assist your husbands and the other lawyers. I remember years ago at a Northern Ireland hearing we had a woman whose husband was murdered—a human rights lawyer named Patrick Finucane—and the bottom line was that by killing and hurting lawyers who are really one of the last protections that citizens have to exercise due process rights and to get their case to resolve grievances, the Chinese Government is going for the jug- ular with this and I think all of us in the Western countries need to realize that our voices have to be raised higher and louder and more effectively than ever before.

And as I said before, every tool that we have in our toolbox needs to be deployed on behalf of your husbands. If the lawyers are silenced, where does any aggrieved party go for help?

Even in a flawed rule of law country like China, still, as your husbands did, you effectuated change. They spoke on behalf of victims and, in some cases, got durable remedy.

So I want to pledge to you that we will all continue. We will make that request of the Trump administration, that you meet with him and with the Vice President, and we will do that immediately by way of letter and by way of phone calls and visits because he needs to look you in the eyes so that when he looks Xi Jinping in the eyes, he has your husband and your interests right there front and center.

So if there is anything you would like to add in terms of what we might have missed, this is your opportunity before we run over to vote.

We are joined by Chairman Mark Meadows. But if there is anything that you would like to add before we conclude. Yes, Ms. Wang.

Ms. WANG. I would like to add on to what we hope the U.S. Government will be doing. My husband, Mr. Tang Jingling, was not participating in anything illegal. These are recognized by both the international community as well as China.

Although he is sentenced to 5 years, I hope that he could be released. Mr. Tang was incarcerated due to his participation in nonviolent civil disobedience, and that resulted in his mother's death. I hope he could come home and visit his elderly father. I hope the U.S. would put extra emphasis and follow these situations of human rights victims or political prisoners and their families who are being persecuted. Because these actions are a violation of human rights, we hope that the U.S. Government will bring these concerns to the Chinese Government. The torturing of all the incarcerated people should stop. They should also stop the persecution against their families, lawyers, and their children. They should also stop their persecution against Christians, Buddhists, Falun Gong, or other religious groups.

Thirdly, I would like to request that the Ambassador to China, Beijing would meet with these victims and families of these victims.

I would also like to ask that before President Trump meets President Xi he would also meet with the families of these victims who reside in the U.S.

Thank you very much.

Ms. LI. My husband's incidents have caused a panic among Taiwanese NGO workers. I hope the United States could strongly pay attention to my husband's incident because all NGO workers around the globe might face the same situation. Thank you.

Mr. SMITH. Thank you.

Without objection, a letter signed by several scores—I think there are about 40 scholars on behalf of your husband—will be made a part of the record. It includes a very diverse group of people, including the former the chief of staff for one of our colleagues, Senator Claiborne Pell, and without objection this will be made a part of the record.

Anybody else before we close? And Mark, would you want to— Ms. Jin.

Ms. JIN. I have another small request. I hope the U.S. Government can raise this issue and ask the Chinese Government to launch an independent investigation on the torture against the lawyers in the 709 cases, and especially the torture method of being drugged. Thank you.

Mr. SMITH. I would like to yield to my good friend and colleague, Mr. Meadows.

Mr. MEADOWS. Mr. Chairman, I want to thank you once again for being a voice for so many people who don't have a voice.

I mean, there is one person out of 435 Members that is a champion and that is not to be disrespectful of my colleagues. I think he would recognize that there is a champion who always wants to make sure that he reaches out, and you are recognized by both Democrats and Republicans, and I just want to say thank you.

But for each one of you, I want to also say that with my colleague opposite from a Democratic perspective but also on the Republican side that we will work in a bipartisan way to address these atrocities and these human rights violations. And I can assure you, at the very highest levels of our Government, they will be made aware of the personal tragedy that you have had to endure and so I just wanted to say that for the record that your testimony here today is meaningful and it will be shared in the appropriate way.

And Mr. Chairman, I yield back.

Mr. SMITH. Mr. Meadows, thank you very much and I really appreciate your work on behalf of human rights that has been longstanding and particularly as a member of this subcommittee. Thank you.

The hearing is adjourned and I thank you all very much.

[Whereupon, at 4 o'clock p.m., the subcommittee was adjourned.]

APPENDIX

<small>MATERIAL SUBMITTED FOR THE RECORD</small>

SUBCOMMITTEE HEARING NOTICE
COMMITTEE ON FOREIGN AFFAIRS
U.S. HOUSE OF REPRESENTATIVES
WASHINGTON, DC 20515-6128

Subcommittee on Africa, Global Health, Global Human Rights, and International Organizations
Christopher H. Smith (R-NJ), Chairman

May 18, 2017

TO: MEMBERS OF THE COMMITTEE ON FOREIGN AFFAIRS

You are respectfully requested to attend an OPEN hearing of the Committee on Foreign Affairs, to be held by the Subcommittee on Africa, Global Health, Global Human Rights, and International Organizations in Room 2172 of the Rayburn House Office Building (and available live on the Committee website at http://www.ForeignAffairs.house.gov):

DATE: Thursday, May 18, 2017

TIME: 2:00 p.m.

SUBJECT: Disappeared, Jailed, and Tortured in China: Wives Petition for Their Husbands' Freedom

WITNESSES: Ms. Li Ching-Yu
                   Spouse of Li Ming-Che

                   Ms. Wang Yanfang
                   Spouse of Tang Jingling

                   Ms. Jin Bianling
                   Spouse of Jiang Tianyong

                   Ms. Chen Guiqiu
                   Spouse of Xie Yang

By Direction of the Chairman

The Committee on Foreign Affairs seeks to make its facilities accessible to persons with disabilities. If you are in need of special accommodations, please call 202/225-5021 at least four business days in advance of the event, whenever practicable. Questions with regard to special accommodations in general (including availability of Committee materials in alternative formats and assistive listening devices) may be directed to the Committee.

COMMITTEE ON FOREIGN AFFAIRS

MINUTES OF SUBCOMMITTEE ON _Africa, Global Health, Global Human Rights, and International Organizations_ HEARING

Day___ _Thursday_ ___Date___ _May 18, 2017_ ___Room_ _2172 Rayburn HOB_

Starting Time ___ _2:01 p.m._ ___Ending Time___ _3:59 p.m._

Recesses | _1_ | (_2:18_ to _2:48_) (___to___) (___to___) (___to___) (___to___) (___to___)

Presiding Member(s)

Rep. Chris Smith

Check all of the following that apply:

Open Session ☑
Executive (closed) Session ☐
Televised ☑

Electronically Recorded (taped) ☑
Stenographic Record ☑

TITLE OF HEARING:

Disappeared, Jailed, and Tortured in China: Wives Petition for Their Husbands' Freedom

---

SUBCOMMITTEE MEMBERS PRESENT:

Rep. Joaquin Castro, Rep. Tom Garrett, Rep. Mark Meadows

NON-SUBCOMMITTEE MEMBERS PRESENT: _(Mark with an * if they are not members of full committee.)_

Rep. Randy Hultgren*

HEARING WITNESSES: Same as meeting notice attached? Yes ☑ No ☐
(if "no", please list below and include title, agency, department, or organization.)

STATEMENTS FOR THE RECORD: _(List any statements submitted for the record.)_

Testimony of Jiang Tianyong from November 10, 2009 hearing, submitted by Rep. Chris Smith
Letter from scholars to Xi Jinping on Li Ming-Che, submitted by Rep. Chris Smith
List of Xie Yang's torturers, submitted by Rep. Chris Smith

TIME SCHEDULED TO RECONVENE _____
or
TIME ADJOURNED ___ _3:59 p.m._

Subcommittee Staff Associate

MATERIAL SUBMITTED FOR THE RECORD BY THE HONORABLE CHRISTOPHER H. SMITH, A REPRESENTATIVE IN CONGRESS FROM THE STATE OF NEW JERSEY, AND CHAIRMAN, SUBCOMMITTEE ON AFRICA, GLOBAL HEALTH, GLOBAL HUMAN RIGHTS, AND INTERNATIONAL ORGANIZATIONS

Testimonies on Violent Implementations of the One-Child Policy in Linyi city, Shandong province, China

By Jiang Tianyong, Beijing Global Law Firm

November 10th 2009

Honorable Congressman, ladies and gentlemen,
Good afternoon!

My name is Jiang Tianyong, I am a lawyer from mainland China. I have taken human rights cases, e.g. the 2005 one-child policy case in Linyi city in Shandong province, the case of Chen Guangcheng, etc. I am not an expert on legal issues of the One-Child Policy, but growing up in mainland China, no one is unaware of the violent implementations of the One-Child Policy.

It is worth mentioning that what I call the "one-child policy" in this testimony is different from internationally-known "family planning" in which a husband and wife make their decision on the number of their family members according to their own will. In 1979, the Chinese government made the One-Child Policy as a basic state policy; on September 1, 2002, the government made the "Law of Population and Family Planning of the People's Republic of China." Later, each province established "Regulations on Populations and Family Planning" in accordance with the law. In this sense, the population and family planning in China is legitimized. Unfortunately, many local family planning officials as well as the executors of the law illegally enforce the law through compulsory abortion, surgical sterilization, etc. The 2005 Linyi case is a typical case and drew international attention at one time. The victim in the case, Mr. Chen Guangcheng, is a blind man. He is oppressed and persecuted by the local government for his legal appeals. He has been in prison for fours years and three month and has not yet been released.

Following is some information we collected in our investigation. Here is the list of investigators: Jiang Tianyong, Cheng Guangcheng, Yuan Weijing, Li Chunfu, Li Jian, Li Heping, Teng Biao, Guo Yushan and a few foreign journalists.

According to the director of Population & Family Planning Bureau in Yinan county in Shandong province, in between March to August of 2005, approximately 7,000 surgical sterilizations were operated. Statistically, there should be 84,000 surgical sterilizations done in Linyi city, Shandong province (includes three districts and nine counties). However, our investigation proved that the surgical sterilizations are far more than 100,000. Most of these surgeries are operated by force after the patients and their families have been beaten, illegally detained and fined.

Fang Zhongxia – a peasant in Linyi city, Fei county, Liang Qiuzhen (county capitol) – suffered persecution with her innocent relatives: three children, a pregnant woman, and her 70-year old mother-in-law. On March 11, 2005, she was forced to take prostaglandins, which induced abortion. The next morning, the seven-mouth fetus was aborted. On the 13th at 9:00 am, she was forced to have sterilization surgery. Her relatives were then finally released.

Hu Bingmei – a peasant in Yinan county, Sunzu town, Shandong province – had high blood pressure and hyper-thyroid. In April of 2005, she was forced to have surgical sterilization. The doctor suggested that it was risky to have the surgery. But the Population and Family Planning officials said, "I said, 'do it.' Just do it!" After the surgery, Ms. Hu had severe sequela: stomachache, shaking, etc, which might last the rest of her life.

On February 28, 2005, Li Juan – a 24-year old pregnant woman from Linyi city, Fei county, Qiuzhen (county capitol) – was forcibly taken to a clinic. The officials held her on the bed and gave her a poisonous shot, despite that her due day was soon. The needle went through her belly to the nine-mouth old fetus. Li said, "At first, I could feel my child was kicking; after a while it stopped." Ten hours later, Li gave birth to a dead baby. The official threw the dead baby into a bucket.

There are many victims like those described above. Many had to escape to avoid being caught. Sometimes, Linyi's Population and Family Planning bureau takes actions at night; the victims dare not to sleep. On June 23, 2005, Chen Guangchen, Li Heping and I investigated at Linyi city, Fei county, Liang Qiuzhen town, Taohuading village in Shandong. We found the village became empty at night. The villagers worked and slept in the field. They have their own "guard." Under the cover of the crops, they report to each other once the officials come. One villager told us, "The officials sneak in and randomly arrest people." On May 9, 2005, lawyer Li Chunfu and I stayed at the home of blind advocate Chen Guangchen. At night, we heard someone banging on our neighbor's door, and then a child burst into screaming. We went out and found about 17 people at the site. They recognized that we are not from that area, and immediately got in the car and left. Chen Guangchen said, "They are the Family Planning officials. They are here to arrest the couple next door."

Many people were involved in persecution. The most unbearable case is that of two siblings who were forced to slap each other in the face. Song Huahou – a 60-year old female, from Linyi city, Fei county, Liangqiu town in Shandong province – and her family were brutally treated only because her daughter-in-law had been pregnant for five months without being reported. Eight of her relatives and two neighbors were beaten savagely. Her 65-old brother was arrested and beaten by the Family Planning officials. Then the officials force Ms. Song and her brother to slap each other on the face. In addition, they charge 100 RMB "education fee" per day. Song begged for mercy and the officials agreed to charge 4000 RMB in total.

The victims of the one-child policy have no one to appeal to. Attorneys that had offered help to them are persecuted. On August 29, 2005, Li Chunfu and I and four other lawyers went to the Linyi city Fei county court to seek help for five victims and to sue the Population and Family Planning officials. On the 30th, we helped file cases for the three victims. The Houfei Court sent us noticed that they dismissed the suit; but the Yinan Court would open a session on October 11 and 12. Later, the Beijing Department of Justice set an investigation on lawyer Li Chunfu and me and demanded for our report on the case. Before we left Beijing for Yinan county, Shandong province, the Beijing Department of Justice strictly forbid us to go. Then we asked lawyer Yang Zaixin to go to Yinan to join the court. On October 11, the Court told Yang, "The session is closed. We will notice you when next session will be." On his way to leave Yinan, Yang Zaixin was beaten by a group of government-hired hooligans. Later, the plaintiffs were forced to withdraw charges. One of the plaintiffs, Hu Bingmei cried over the phone, "This is an evil government. They threatened me to withdraw charges. If not, they will kill my children on their way to school. But I will disappoint Chen Guangchen and all the lawyers if I stopped action."

The one-child policy issue is national. In May 2007, the Bobai event caused 50,000 people to protest in Guangxi Province. The protest increased and reached to Yulin city in Guangxi province and some other places. According to news reports, there was a family planning campaign in May 2009 in Xianyou county, Fujian province, where the Family Planning officials illegally arrested and forced pregnant women to have surgical sterilization. The local officials' explanation of their dehumanizing acts is that they are afraid to lose their jobs.

In mainland China, a married couple has to have a Birth Permit to give birth to their first child; once they have a child, a couple must have Pregnancy Permit and Birth Permit to have a second child. Otherwise, pregnant women will have to confront compulsory abortion. Nowadays, such tragedies caused by this family planning enforcement are continuing.

Thank you!

Xi Jinping, President of the People's Republic of China
Zhongnanhai,
No. 174 Xi Chang'an Jie,
Beijing 100017 China

April 16th 2017

Dear President Xi Jinping,

The undersigned are international scholars and writers from nations around the globe. We hereby express to you our deep concern about the disappearance of Mr. Li Ming-che (李明哲) from Taiwan. Mr. Li is a respected human rights worker, who in the past worked for the Democratic Progressive Party, and who is now a program manager at Wenshan Community College in Taipei.

Mr. Li disappeared on Sunday March 19th 2017 while he entered China from Macau. It wasn't until March 29th that PRC authorities stated in a routine press conference that Mr. Li had been detained under circumstances that remain unexplained. This failure to notify the family within 24 hours violated both Mr. Li's human rights and the Cross-Strait Joint Crime-Fighting and Judicial Mutual Assistance Agreement (海峽兩岸共同打擊犯罪及司法互助協議).

We are particularly concerned by the fact that the Taiwan Affairs Office announced on March 29th 2017 that Li was being investigated on suspicion of "involvement in activities that threaten national security." We find this allegation to be at severe odds with the fact that Mr. Li is a human rights worker who attempted to enhance communication between people in Taiwan and China.

We are also disturbed by the fact that on April 10th 2017, the Chinese authorities prevented Mr. Li's wife, Li Ching-yu (李淨瑜), from boarding a flight to Beijing by cancelling her "Taiwan compatriot travel document." This action also disregarded the human rights of this young couple and raises substantial doubts about the intentions of the Chinese authorities.

As is becoming clear, Mr. Li's arrest and detention is detrimental to the mutual trust that is very much needed between Taiwan and China. We therefore urge you to assist in the speedy release of Mr. Li and his safe return to Taiwan. Any lengthy detention or legal procedure will damage China's image, not only in Taiwan, but in countries around the world that uphold due process of law and human rights.

Respectfully yours,

1. Clive Ansley, Lawyer, Vancouver, BC, Canada

2. Joseph A. Bosco, Georgetown University (ret), Washington DC

3. Richard C. Bush, The Brookings Institution, Washington DC

4. Coen Blaauw, Formosan Association for Public Affairs, Washington DC

5. Jie Chen, University of Western Australia, Perth, Australia

6. Wen-yen Chen, University of the District of Columbia, Washington DC

7. Louisa Chiang, independent researcher, Washington DC

8. Michael Danielsen, Taiwan Corner, Copenhagen, Denmark

9. Evan Dawley, Goucher College, Towson MD

10. June Teufel Dreyer, University of Miami, Coral Gables FL

11. Feng Chongyi, University of Technology Sydney, Australia

12. Carl Ford, National Park University, Park AR

13. Brock Freeman, American Citizens for Taiwan, Seattle WA

14. Edward Friedman, University of Wisconsin, Madison WI

15. Mark Harrison, University of Tasmania, Australia

16. Michael R. Hoare, SOAS, University of London, UK

17. Thomas G. Hughes, former chief of staff senator Claiborne Pell, Washington DC

18. Victoria Hui, University of Norte Dame, IN

19. Michael A. Hunzeker, George Mason University, Fairfax VA

20. Saša Istenič, University of Ljubljana, Slovenia

21. J. Bruce Jacobs, Monash University, Melbourne, Australia

22. Paul Jobin, University of Paris Diderot, France

23. Richard C. Kagan, Hamline University (ret), St. Paul MN

24. Michael Y.M. Kau, Brown University (ret), Providence RI

25. Han-jung Ko, Central Michigan University, Mt. Pleasant MI

26. Raymond Kuo, Fordham University, Bronx NY

27. Lut Lams, Catholic University Leuven, Brussels, Belgium

28. Perry Link, University of California, Riverside CA

29. Ben Read, University of California, Santa Cruz CA

30. Shawna Yang Ryan, University of Hawaii, Manoa HI

31. Michael Scanlon, Shih Chien University, Kaohsiung, Taiwan

32. David Schak, Griffith University, Queensland, Australia

33. Jonathan Schwartz, State University of New York, New Paltz NY

34. Scott Simon, University of Ottawa, Canada

35. Michael Stainton, Taiwanese Human Rights Association, Toronto, Canada

36. William A. Stanton, National Tsinghua University, Hsinchu, Taiwan

37. Peter Tague, Georgetown University Law Center, Washington DC

38. Kharis A. Templeman, Stanford University, Stanford CA

39. Ross Terrill, Harvard University, Cambridge MA

40. John J. Tkacik, International Assessment and Strategy Center, Alexandria VA

41. Arthur Waldron, University of Pennsylvania, Philadelphia PA

42. Gerrit van der Wees, George Mason University, Fairfax VA

43. Jack F. Williams, Michigan State University (ret), East Lansing MI

44. Yenna Wu, University of California, Riverside CA

Hanji translation of the letter:

習近平總統鈞鑒：

這封信是由來自世界各地的國際學者和作家共同署名。有關台灣的李明哲在中國失蹤這個案件，我們在此向您們表達深度的關切。李明哲是受尊敬的人權工作者，他曾經當過民進黨的黨工，目前是台北市文山社區大學的職員。

李明哲三月十九日從澳門入境中國後即失蹤，下落不明。中國當局等到三月二十七日在一個例行的記者會中才提到李明哲被扣押的消息，而被捕的原因並沒有說明清楚。中國當局沒有在二十四小時之內通知家屬，此舉明顯的侵犯李明哲的人權和違反「海峽兩岸共同打擊犯罪及司法互助協議」的規定。

我們特別關心的是中國的國務院台灣事務辦公室於二月二十九日宣布李明哲是因為「涉嫌從事危害國家安全的活動」而被拘禁。這個指控完全不符合事實。因為李先生是位人權工作者，他只是想儘力促進台灣和中國兩岸人民的交流。

讓我們憂心的是中國當局為了阻止李明哲妻子李淨瑜飛到北京而在登機前註銷她的台胞証。此舉不但忽視李明哲夫婦的人權，也讓人質疑中國當局的誠意。

李明哲的逮捕和拘禁很明顯的損害兩岸人民非常需要的互信。我們敦請您們從中協助儘速釋放李明哲，讓他安全回台與家人團聚。李明哲拘禁時間再拖延，或訴諸法律程序只會傷害中國的國家形象，這個傷害不只是在台灣而已，也會傷害中國在國際上的形象，尤其是在以法治和人權治國的國家，中國的國家形象將會更加受損。

尚此

順頌

MATERIAL SUBMITTED FOR THE RECORD BY THE HONORABLE CHRISTOPHER H. SMITH, A REPRESENTATIVE IN CONGRESS FROM THE STATE OF NEW JERSEY, AND CHAIRMAN, SUBCOMMITTEE ON AFRICA, GLOBAL HEALTH, GLOBAL HUMAN RIGHTS, AND INTERNATIONAL ORGANIZATIONS

Changsha Municipal Domestic Security Detachment

1) Captain Li Kewei

2) Lieutenant Wang Dehua

3) Captain Wang Tietuo of the Sixth Brigade

4) Lieutenant Zhu Heng of the Sixth Brigade

5) Instructor Ye Yun of the Sixth Brigade

Hunan Domestic Security Corps

6) Li Feng

Dongkou County Domestic Security Corps: public security officers

7) Captain Xie Leshi

8) Zhou Lang

9) Yin Zhuo

10) Qu Ke

11) Li Yang

12) Zhou Yi

13) Zhuang Xiaoliang

Hunan Provincial People's Procuratorate, Second Public Prosecution Department;

14) Department Director Liu Xiaohong

15) Procurators Duan Xiaolong,

16) Jiang Bin,

17) Li Zhiming

18) Wang Zhiyong

19) Fang Hui

20) Hu Yongchao

21) Li Weining

22) Bailiff Yuan Jin

www.ingramcontent.com/pod-product-compliance
Lightning Source LLC
Chambersburg PA
CBHW081239280526
45787CB00006B/2720